Stewardship
A Disciple's Response

A Pastoral Letter on Stewardship

Tenth Anniversary Edition

includes

To Be a Christian Steward

A Summary of the U.S. Bishops' Pastoral Letter on Stewardship

and

Stewardship and Development in Catholic Dioceses and Parishes: A Resource Manual

Our Sunday Visitor
Huntington, Indiana

United States Conference of Catholic Bishops

The original document *Stewardship: A Disciple's Response* was developed by the Ad Hoc Committee on Stewardship of the United States Conference of Catholic Bishops (USCCB). It was approved by the full body of U.S. Catholic bishops at its November 1992 General Meeting. The companion document *Stewardship and Development in Catholic Dioceses and Parishes: A Resource Manual* was developed as a resource by the Ad Hoc Committee on Stewardship in 1996. The preface to the tenth anniversary edition was approved by the full body of U.S. Catholic bishops at its November 2002 General Meeting, and this edition has been authorized for publication by the undersigned.

Msgr. William P. Fay
General Secretary, USCCB

Grateful acknowledgment is extended to the National Catholic Development Conference and the National Catholic Stewardship Council, whose financial support has enabled this project to be undertaken.

In 2001 the National Conference of Catholic Bishops and United States Catholic Conference became the United States Conference of Catholic Bishops.

Current printing, 2023, published by OSV, Our Sunday VIsitor, Inc., 200 Noll Plaza,Huntington, IN 46750; www.osv.com; 1-800-348-2440

ISBN: 978-1-63966-188-6 (Inventory No. T2885)

PRINTED IN THE UNITED STATES OF AMERICA

Contents

Preface

"ONCE ONE CHOOSES TO BECOME A DISCIPLE OF JESUS CHRIST, STEWARDSHIP IS NOT AN OPTION."

With these words, Bishop John J. McRaith, an original member of the U.S. Catholic bishops' Ad Hoc Committee on Stewardship, summarized succinctly the heart of the 1992 pastoral letter *Stewardship: A Disciple's Response*. Ten years after its publication, the pastoral letter's challenge that we embrace stewardship as an expression of discipleship with the "power to change how we understand and live out our lives" continues to engage lay people, religious men and women, priests, deacons, and bishops.[1] This challenge is just as powerful today as in 1992, as a new generation of Catholics is introduced to the biblical concept of stewardship and embraces "the call to follow Jesus and imitate his way of life."[2]

In the words of the late Archbishop Thomas Murphy, the first chairman of the Ad Hoc Committee, "How do we develop among ourselves, our priests, seminarians, and lay people a spirituality of giving that offers a biblical concept of stewardship?" This tenth anniversary edition of *Stewardship: A Disciple's Response* can serve as a gospel blueprint with which to develop and expand this concept to build the kingdom of God. As with all things pertaining to the Gospel, stewardship is fundamentally the work of the Spirit in our lives. When we accept our lives as sheer gifts, the Spirit can use us as apt instruments for spreading the Gospel. Wherever the Spirit works, there is joy. Good stewards are always the joyful bearers of the Good News of Salvation.

Much has been accomplished with stewardship as a way of life in the contemporary Church. Since 1992, archdiocesan and diocesan offices and directors of stewardship have multiplied across the nation, and every year increasing numbers of parishes introduce stewardship and the spirituality of giving. An increasing international attention on stewardship has raised new approaches toward stewardship awareness. We can observe and learn from Catholic communities in different countries who are eagerly implementing the concepts of the pastoral letter in terms of their own traditions and cultures.

The stewardship pastoral letter strongly reflects the core of the Easter message of the earliest Christian community: "We have seen the Lord!" (Jn 20:25). Stewardship always starts with the personal experience of the Risen Christ in our midst and in our hearts. It is a vocation to discipleship. The following of Christ as a disciple entails a personal response, and this call can result in a positive impact on our faith communities.

Discipleship requires the surrender of ourselves through grace and choice to Jesus Christ: "Mature disciples make a conscious, firm decision, carried out in action, to be followers of Jesus Christ no matter the cost to themselves."[3] A disciple is both a learner and a companion of Jesus Christ, as well as one open to the movement of the Holy Spirit towards a gracious generosity of heart. The authentic disciple regards all he or she is and possesses as gifts and blessings and realizes the need to share those gifts and blessings with others for the sake of the kingdom of God.

Stewardship: A Disciple's Response describes conversion as "committing one's very self to the Lord." The letter continues, "Stewardship is an expression of discipleship, with the power to change how we understand and live out our lives."[4] Good stewards live with joy and gratitude for the blessings they have received—including those that have multiplied through diligence and hard work. Indeed, good stewards live in communion with Christ and through Christ and the Spirit strive to return all gifts to the Father "*with an increase*." The stewardship pastoral letter spells out this giving of ourselves in its fourth section, entitled "Stewards of the Church," which starts with the reality of the Church as God's gift: "The New Covenant in and through Christ—the reconciliation he effects between humankind and God—forms a community: the new People of God, the Body of Christ, the Church."[5]

Individuals compose collectively the Body of Christ; therefore, disciples of Jesus Christ are stewards of the Church because stewardship is the personal responsibility of each one of the baptized. The pastoral letter quotes from St. Paul's letter to the Corinthians: "To each individual the manifestation of the Spirit is given for some benefit (1 Cor 12:7)."[6]

Examples of the works, services, and ministries of the good steward enumerated in the stewardship letter include the following:

- Evangelization and witness to the Gospel
- Catechesis and faith formation
- Parent stewardship of the domestic church
- Stewardship of simplicity of life
- Stewardship for ecology of the globe
- Lay witness in the marketplace and institutions
- Financial accountability in personal and parochial affairs
- Stewardship of collegiality and collaboration in parish life and ministries
- Stewardship of social justice and the work for peace

Stewardship, then, is all-encompassing. It provides a place for the simplest individual gesture of kindness as well as stewardship communities working for systemic justice and peace. Stewardship flowing from a personal and communal relationship to Christ holds a particular attraction to people. It is, ultimately, the pull and the power of the Gospel come alive in our times and circumstances.

This pastoral letter speaks eloquently to youth, whose idealism and energy are needed and welcome in the challenge of stewardship. Stewardship can lead youth and young adults to a more mature understanding of their lives as a vocation—as a call to serve Christ and the Church as a layperson, religious, deacon, or priest. When we accept God's gifts gratefully, the experience invariably leads to new depths of discerning how the Spirit leads people to a further response to God's call.

The publication of *Go and Make Disciples*, the U.S. bishops' pastoral letter on evangelization, in the same year as the pastoral letter on stewardship, enhanced Catholics' understanding of the

Church's mission as including both evangelization and stewardship. Together these two documents emphasize conversion of heart as vital to the overall mission of the Church. In the letter on evangelization, we read, "Conversion is the change of our lives that comes about through the power of the Holy Spirit. All who accept the Gospel undergo change as we continually put on the mind of Christ by rejecting sin and becoming more faithful disciples in his Church."[7] The stewardship pastoral letter affirms the same truth: "Beginning in conversion, change of mind and heart, this commitment is expressed not in a single action, nor even in a number of actions over a period of time, but in an entire way of life."[8]

Stewardship: A Disciple's Response describes and fosters the gospel spirituality of sharing. At the beginning of the letter we read, "This pastoral letter recognizes the importance of church support, including the sharing of time, talent, and treasure. But it situates church support in its broader context—what it means to be a disciple of Jesus Christ."[9] This way of life has its center and source of strength in the Eucharist: "The Eucharist is the great sign and agent of this expansive communion of charity. . . . Here people enjoy a unique union with Christ and, in him, with one another."[10]

Christ and the Holy Spirit lead us to the Father in our liturgical life of praise and thanksgiving. We bring to the Eucharist all we are and all we have shared as stewards. As the elements of bread and wine are changed into the Body and Blood of Christ through the action of the Spirit, we also become more deeply transformed as disciples and stewards.

This pastoral letter has served as an indispensable way to communicate a vision and extend an invitation to Christian people to "*grasp the fact that they are no less than 'God's co-workers' (1 Cor 3:9), with their own particular share in his creative, redemptive, and sanctifying work.*"[11] Everyone who has studied and acted on this letter knows that it will continue to attract and guide countless new co-workers to the Church's mission.

On this tenth anniversary we express gratitude to God for the wisdom of those who authored *Stewardship: A Disciple's Response*. We thank the countless people who as disciples have spread the concepts and gospel values of the pastoral letter to the daily life of the People of God and have provided for the needs of the Church.

Bishop Sylvester D. Ryan
Chairman
Ad Hoc Committee on Stewardship

Notes

1 See page 5 of this edition.
2 Ibid., 8.
3 Ibid., 5.
4 Ibid.
5 Ibid., 31.
6 Ibid.
7 United States Conference of Catholic Bishops, *Go and Make Disciples: A National Plan and Strategy for Catholic Evangelization in the United States: Tenth Anniversay English and Spanish Edition* (Washington, DC: USCCB, 2002), no. 12.
8 See page 5 of this edition.
9 Ibid., 6.
10 Ibid., 34.
11 Ibid., 40 (italics added).

Stewardship

A Disciple's Response

AS EACH ONE HAS RECEIVED A GIFT,

USE IT TO SERVE ONE ANOTHER

AS GOOD STEWARDS OF GOD'S VARIED GRACE.

(1 PT 4:10)

Introduction

Three convictions in particular underlie what we say in this pastoral letter.

1. Mature disciples make
a conscious, firm decision,
carried out in action,
to be followers of Jesus Christ
no matter the cost to themselves.

2. Beginning in conversion,
change of mind and heart,
this commitment
is expressed not in a single action,
nor even in a number of actions
over a period of time,
but in an entire way of life.
It means committing
one's very self
to the Lord.

3. Stewardship is an expression of discipleship,
with the power to change
how we understand and live out our lives.
Disciples
who practice stewardship
recognize God
as the origin of life,
the giver of freedom,
the source of all they have and are and will be. They are deeply aware of the truth that "The Lord's are the earth and its fullness; the world and those who dwell in it" (Ps 24:1). They know themselves to be recipients and caretakers of God's many gifts.
They are grateful
for what they have received
and eager to cultivate their gifts
out of love for God
and one another.

THE CHALLENGE

In some ways
it may be harder
to be a Christian steward today
than at times in the past.

Although religious faith is a strong force
in the lives of many Americans,
our country's dominant secular culture
often contradicts the values
of the Judaeo-Christian tradition.
This is a culture
in which destructive "isms"—
materialism,
relativism,
hedonism,
individualism,
consumerism—
exercise seductive, powerful influences.
There is a strong tendency
to privatize faith,
to push it to the margins of society,
confining it to people's hearts
or, at best, their homes,
while excluding it from the marketplace of ideas
where social policy is formed
and men and women acquire their view of life
and its meaning.

THE CHOICE

Christians
are part of this culture,
influenced by it
in many ways.

In recent decades
many Catholics in particular
have entered into
the mainstream of American society.
That has been
a remarkable achievement.
Often, though,
this process also has widened
the "split" between faith and life
which Vatican II saw as one of
"the more serious errors
of our age" (*Gaudium et Spes*, no. 43).
Thus American Catholicism itself
has taken on
some of the less attractive values
of the secular culture.

For example,
although religious people often speak about community,
individualism infects the religious experience
of many persons.
Parishes,
dioceses,
and church institutions
appear impersonal and alienating
in the eyes of many.
Evangelization
is not the priority it should be.
How to use people's gifts and charisms,
how to empower the laity,
how to recognize the role of women,
how to affirm racial, cultural, and ethnic minorities, how to overcome poverty and oppression—
these and countless other issues
remain vexing questions,
as well as
opportunities.

Also,
while many Catholics are generous
in giving of themselves
and their resources
to the Church,
others do not respond
to the needs
in proportion
to what they possess.
The result now is a lack of resources
which seriously hampers
the Church's ability
to carry out its mission
and obstructs
people's growth as disciples.

This pastoral letter recognizes the importance
of church support,
including the sharing of time, talent, and treasure.
But it situates
church support
in its broader context—
what it means to be
a disciple
of Jesus Christ.

This also
is the context
of stewardship.
Generous sharing of resources,
including money,
is central to its practice,

and church support
is a necessary part of this.
Essentially,
it means
helping the Church's mission
with money, time, and personal resources of all kinds. This sharing is not an option for Catholics
who understand
what membership in the Church involves.
It is a serious duty.
It is a consequence
of the faith
which Catholics profess
and celebrate.

This pastoral letter initiates
a long-term, continuing process
encouraging people
to examine and interiorize
stewardship's implications.
At the start of this process
it is important to lay out
a comprehensive view of stewardship
—a vision of a sharing, generous, accountable way
of life rooted in Christian discipleship—
which people can take to heart
and apply to the circumstances
of their lives.
Concentrating on one specific obligation of stewardship, even one as important as church support,
could make it harder
—even impossible—
for people to grasp the vision.
It could imply
that when the bishops
get serious about stewardship,
what they really mean is
simply giving money.

THE VISION

Jesus' invitation
to follow him
is addressed to people
of every time and condition.
Here and now
it is addressed to us—
Catholic citizens
of a wealthy, powerful nation
facing many questions
about its identity and role
in the waning years
of a troubled century,
members of a community of faith
blessed with many human
and material resources
yet often uncertain
about how to sustain
and use them.

As bishops, we wish
to present a vision
that suits
the needs and problems
of the Church in our country today
and speaks to those
who practice Christian stewardship
in their particular circumstances.

What we say here
is directed to ourselves
as much as to you
who read these words.
As bishops,
we recognize our obligation

to be models of stewardship
in all aspects of our lives.
We must be stewards
in our prayer and worship,
in how we fulfill
our pastoral duties,
in our custody of the Church's
doctrine, spiritual resources, personnel, and funds,
in our lifestyle and use of time,
and even in such matters
as the attention we give to
personal health and recreation.

As we ask you to respond
to the challenge of stewardship,
we pray that we also
will be open to the grace to respond.
We pray that the Holy Spirit, whose gracious action conforms us to Jesus Christ and to the Church,
will enlighten us all and help us to renew our commitment as the Lord's disciples and as stewards of his bountiful gifts.

THE PLAN OF THE PASTORAL LETTER

The pastoral letter proceeds according to the following plan.

I. The Call

Stewardship is part of discipleship. But Christian discipleship begins with vocation, the call to follow Jesus and imitate his way of life. The letter therefore begins with vocation. Then it presents a very general overview of stewardship, considered in the context of discipleship, noting that people first of all are stewards of the personal vocations they receive from God. Discipleship and the practice of stewardship constitute a way of life that is both privileged and challenging.

II. Jesus' Way

Next, the pastoral letter focuses more closely on the idea of stewardship, relying on the teaching and life of Jesus to probe its meaning. It considers the implications for disciples of Jesus engaged in stewardship. One of these is that all are called to evangelize, to share the Good News with others. And what is the reward to which good stewards can look forward? The answer is perfect fulfillment in God's Kingdom—a kingdom already present, real but imperfect, in this world, which Jesus' disciples help bring to its full reality by the practice of stewardship.

III. Living as a Steward

Having reflected in general terms upon Christian life considered from the point of view of discipleship and stewardship, the letter turns to the content of this way of life. It considers the content of life in relation to two human activities that are fundamental to the Christian vocation. The first is collaborating with God in the work of creation. The second is cooperating with God in the work of redemption. Both lie at the very heart of Christian stewardship in its deepest meaning.

IV. Stewards of the Church

The pastoral letter next considers the community of faith, the People of God, which is formed by the New Covenant in and through Christ. Each member of the Church shares in responsibility for its mission; each is called to practice stewardship of the Church. Christians also are called to look outward and to place themselves at the service of the entire human community, especially those who are most in need. The Eucharist is both the sign and the agent of this expansive communion of charity.

V. The Christian Steward

The letter closes with a brief portrait or profile of the Christian steward, drawn from the New Testament. In a special way, the Blessed Virgin is the model of Christian discipleship and of the practice of Christian stewardship as it is understood here. Do we also wish to be disciples of Jesus Christ and to live in this way?

Who is a Christian disciple? One who responds to Christ's call, follows Jesus, and shapes his or her life in imitation of Christ's. Who is a Christian steward? One who receives God's gifts gratefully, cherishes and tends them in a responsible and accountable manner, shares them in justice and love with others, and returns them with increase to the Lord.

Genesis tells us that God placed the first human beings in a garden to practice stewardship there—"to cultivate and care for it" (Gn 2:15). The world remains a kind of garden (or workshop, as some would prefer to say) entrusted to the care of men and women for God's glory and the service of humankind. In its simplest yet deepest sense, this is the Christian stewardship of which the pastoral letter speaks.

For Reflection and Discussion

1. Do you agree with the bishops' reasons for writing and publishing a pastoral letter on stewardship?

2. Were you surprised (or, perhaps, disappointed) by the bishops' "high road" discourse on stewardship, seemingly unrelated to pressing financial problems in the contemporary Church?

3. Would you add to or subtract from the bishops' three basic convictions that underlie the whole pastoral letter?

4. Do you agree or disagree that in our United States' culture materialism, relativism, hedonism, individualism, consumerism, and other evil "isms" are at work and influential?

5. In your life, what may be (or actually is) the major obstacle to practicing stewardship in the context of Christian discipleship?

6. If you were encouraged to advise the bishops on how to be faithful stewards, what advice would you offer?

7. What does the word of God say to you regarding discipleship and stewardship? Share your reflections with others.

> Thus should one regard us: as servants of Christ and stewards of the mysteries of God. Now it is of course required of stewards that they be found trustworthy. (1 Cor 4:1-2)
>
> If a brother or sister has nothing to wear and has no food for the day, and one of you says to them, "Go in peace, keep warm, and eat well," but you do not give them the necessities of the body, what good is it? So also faith of itself, if it does not have works, is dead. (Jas 2:15-17)
>
> The Lord replied, "Who, then, is the faithful and prudent steward whom the master will put in charge of his servants to distribute [the] food allowance at the proper time? Blessed is that servant whom his master on arrival finds doing so. Truly, I say to you, he will put him in charge of all his property." (Lk 12:42-44)

8. Comment on the following passages:

> The disciples are not only to learn humility and fraternal love, they must actually participate in the mystery. (Romano Guardini)
>
> But the fundamental law of discipleship is this: being-with-Jesus means learning to go where Jesus is. Being-with-Jesus should eventually bring us to identify with the world and the people with whom Jesus identifies himself. (William Reiser)
>
> Being a steward means living with trust in God's generosity and a responsible tending of that which God has entrusted to us. It also means the fair, just, and righteous sharing of resources with others. (United Church of Christ, *Christian Faith: Personal Stewardship and Economic Sharing*)
>
> It is indeed an exacting discipline to try to be the Church in a culture such as ours. All the assumptions upon which we could rely, which we could take for granted in other times and places, are missing. It is therefore necessary to demonstrate, in the face of cultural skepticism, what a community of loyal and committed believers is really like. (Robert N. Bellah)

I. The Call

As our concept of stewardship continues to evolve after twelve years of marriage, we are grateful for the people who have challenged us from the beginning to embrace fully Christ's teachings. They weren't always telling us the things we wanted to hear, but we feel blessed that we were able to work through the initial frustrations of committing the best portion of our time, talent, and treasure to the Church. It's difficult to separate ourselves from the demands and possessions of the world, but there's a tremendous amount of peace that comes from every decision we make for Christ and his will for us. We can't overstate the powerful impact the lifestyle has had on our marriage and three children.

—Tom and LaNell Lilly
Owensboro, Kentucky

THE DISCIPLE'S VOCATION

The Christian vocation is essentially a call to be a disciple of Jesus. Stewardship is part of that. Even more to the point, however, Christians are called to be good stewards of the personal vocations they receive. Each of us must discern, accept, and live out joyfully and generously the commitments, responsibilities, and roles to which God calls him or her. The account of the calling of the first disciples, near the beginning of John's Gospel, sheds light on these matters.

John the Baptist is standing with two of his disciples—Andrew and, according to tradition, the future evangelist John—when Jesus passes by. "Behold," John the Baptist exclaims, "the Lamb of God!" Wondering at these words, his companions follow Christ.

"What are you looking for?" Jesus asks them. "Rabbi," they say, "Where are you staying?" "Come and you will see." They spend the day with him, enthralled by his words and by the power of his personality.

Deeply moved by this experience, Andrew seeks out his brother Simon and brings him to Jesus. The Lord greets him: "You will be called Kephas"—Rock. The next day, encountering Philip, Jesus tells him: "Follow me." Philip finds his friend Nathanael and, challenging his skepticism, introduces him to the Lord. Soon Nathanael too is convinced: "Rabbi, you are the Son of God; you are the King of Israel."

This fast-paced narrative at the beginning of John's Gospel (see Jn 1:35-50) teaches a number of lessons. For our purposes, two stand out.

One is the personal nature of a call from Jesus Christ. He does not summon disciples as a faceless crowd but as unique individuals. "How do you know me?" Nathanael asks. "Before Philip called you," Jesus answers, "I saw you under the fig tree." He knows people's personal histories, their strengths and weaknesses, their destinies; he has a purpose in mind for each one.

This purpose is individual vocation. "Only in the unfolding of the history of our lives and its events," says Pope John Paul II, "is the eternal plan of God revealed to each of us" (*Christifideles Laici*, no. 58). Every human life, every personal vocation, is unique.

And yet the vocations of all Christians do have elements in common. One of these is the call to be a disciple. In fact, we might say that to be disciples—to follow Christ and try to live his life as our own—*is* the common vocation of Christians; discipleship in this sense *is* Christian life.

The other lesson that John's narrative makes clear is that people do not hear the Lord's call in isolation from one another. Other disciples help mediate their vocations to them, and they in turn are meant to mediate the Lord's call to others. Vocations are communicated, discerned, accepted, and lived out within a community of faith which is a community of disciples (cf. Pope John Paul II, *Redemptor Hominis*, no. 21); its members try to help one another hear the Lord's voice and respond.

RESPONDING TO THE CALL

Jesus not only calls people to him but also forms them and sends them out in his service (cf. Mt 10:5ff.; Mk 6:7ff.; Lk 9:1ff.). Being sent on a mission is a consequence of being a disciple. Whoever wants to follow Christ will have much work to do on his behalf—announcing the Good News and serving others as Jesus did.

Jesus' call is urgent. He does not tell people to follow him at some time in the future but here and now—at *this* moment, in *these* circumstances. There can be no delay. "Go and proclaim the kingdom of God. . . . No one who sets a hand to the plow and looks to what was left behind is fit for the kingdom of God" (Lk 9:60, 62).

But a person can say no to Christ. Consider the wealthy and good young man who approaches Jesus asking how to lead an even better life. Sell your goods, Jesus tells him; give to the poor, and follow me. "When the young man heard this statement, he went away sad, for he had many possessions" (Mt 19:22).

JESUS NOT ONLY CALLS PEOPLE TO HIM BUT ALSO FORMS THEM AND SENDS THEM OUT IN HIS SERVICE.

Attachment to possessions is always more or less a problem, both for individuals and for the community of faith. In *The Long Loneliness* (New York: Doubleday/ Image Books, 1959), written years after she became a Catholic, Dorothy Day recalls the "scandal" of encountering a worldly Church—or, more properly, the worldliness of some Catholics: "businesslike priests . . . collective wealth . . . lack of sense of responsibility for the poor." She concludes: "There was plenty of charity but too little justice" (140).

THE CALL TO STEWARDSHIP

Becoming a disciple of Jesus Christ leads naturally to the practice of stewardship. These linked realities, discipleship and stewardship, then make up the fabric of a Christian life in which each day is lived in an intimate, personal relationship with the Lord.

This Christ-centered way of living has its beginning in Baptism, the sacrament of faith. As Vatican II remarks, all Christians are "bound to show forth, by the example of their lives and by the witness of their speech," that new life of faith which begins in Baptism and is strengthened by the power of the Holy Spirit in Confirmation (*Ad Gentes*, no. 11). Faith joins individuals and the community of Jesus' followers in intimacy with their Lord and leads them to live as his disciples. Union with Christ gives rise to a sense of solidarity and common cause between the disciples and the Lord and also among the disciples themselves.

Refracted through the prisms of countless individual vocations, this way of life embodies and expresses the one mission of Christ: to do God's will, to proclaim the Good News of salvation, to heal the afflicted, to care for one's sisters and brothers, to give life—life to the full—as Jesus did.

Following Jesus is the work of a lifetime. At every step forward, one is challenged to go further in accepting and loving God's will. Being a disciple is not just something else to do, alongside many other things suitable for Christians; it is a total way of life and requires continuing conversion.

Stewardship plays an important role in the lives of people who seek to follow Christ. In particular, as we have said, Christians must be stewards of their personal vocations, for it is these that show how, according to the circumstances of their individual lives, God wants them to cherish and serve a broad range of interests and concerns: life and health, along with their own intellectual and spiritual well-being and that of others; material goods and resources; the natural environment;

the cultural heritage of humankind—indeed, the whole rich panoply of human goods, both those already realized and those whose realization depends upon the present generation or upon generations yet to come. Catholics have a duty, too, to be stewards of their Church: that community of disciples, that Body of Christ, of which they, individually and together, are the members, and in which "if one part suffers, all the parts suffer with it; if one part is honored, all the parts share its joy" (1 Cor 12:26).

THE COST OF DISCIPLESHIP

The way of discipleship is privileged beyond any other. Jesus says: "I came so that they might have life and have it more abundantly" (Jn 10:10). But discipleship is not an easy way. "If you wish to come after me," Jesus also says, "you must deny yourself and take up your cross daily and follow me. For if you wish to save your life you will lose it, but if you lose your life for my sake you will save it" (Lk 9:23-24).

The Lord's way is not a way of comfortable living or of what Dietrich Bonhoeffer, in *The Cost of Discipleship*, scornfully calls "cheap grace." This is not real grace but an illusion. It is what happens when people approach the following of Christ as a way to pleasant experiences and feeling good. Bonhoeffer contrasts this with "costly" grace. It is costly because it calls us to follow, and grace because it calls us to follow *Jesus Christ*. It is costly because it requires a disciple for Jesus' sake to put aside the craving for domination, possession, and control, and grace because it confers true liberation and eternal life. It is costly, finally, because it condemns sin, and grace because it justifies the sinner.

But all this is very general. To understand and practice this way of life, people need models to imitate. These exist in abundance in the holy women and men who have gone before us in the faith; while our supreme source of guidance is found in the person and teaching of Jesus. Let us reflect on what he tells us about stewardship.

For Reflection and Discussion

1. Mr. and Mrs. Lilly speak about "giving" the best portion of their time, talent, and treasure to the Church. What might be your "best portion"?

2. In what sense is stewardship more radical than the sharing of time, talent, and money?

3. If you believe that you are "called," what human, personal experience has reinforced your faith in the call?

4. What are some of the reasons why you might hesitate to respond to the Lord's call?

5. Do you feel that to be a faithful steward you will have to do it alone, or can you count on moral support from other sources? Which ones?

6. If you were to be an ideal Christian steward—with the help of God's grace, of course—what would it cost you in terms of personal sacrifice and hardship?

7. What does the word of God say to you about our vocation to become disciples and stewards of the mysteries of God? Share your reflections with others.

> The word of the LORD came to me thus:
> Before I formed you in the womb I knew you,
> before you were born I dedicated you,
> a prophet to the nations I appointed you.
> "Ah, Lord God!" I said,
> "I know not how to speak; I am too young."
>
> But the LORD answered me,
> Say not, "I am too young."
> To whomever I send you, you shall go;
> whatever I command you, you shall speak.
> Have no fear before them,
> because I am with you to deliver you,
> says the LORD. (Jer 1:4-8)
>
> For I am the least of the apostles, not fit to be called an apostle, because I persecuted the church of God. But by the grace of God I am what I am, and his grace to me has not been ineffective. Indeed, I have toiled harder than all of them; not I, however, but the grace of God [that is] with me. Therefore, whether it be I or they, so we preach and so you believed. (1 Cor 15:9-11)

Here is my servant whom I uphold,
    my chosen one with whom I am pleased,
  Upon whom I have put my spirit;
    he shall bring forth justice to the nations,
  Not crying out, not shouting,
    not making his voice heard in the street.
  A bruised reed he shall not break,
    and a smoldering wick he shall not quench.
    (Is 42:1-3)

8. Comment on the following passages:

In the various types and duties of life, one and the same holiness is cultivated by all who are moved by the Spirit of God, and who obey the voice of the Father, worshiping God and Father in spirit and in truth. These souls follow the poor Christ, the humble and cross-bearing Christ, in order to be made worthy of being partakers in His glory. Every person should walk unhesitatingly according to his own personal gifts and duties in the path of a living faith which arouses hope and works through charity. (Vatican Council II, *Lumen Gentium*, no. 41)

Without a vocation, man's existence would be meaningless. We have been created to bear the responsibility God has entrusted us with. Though different, each man should fulfill his specific vocation and shoulder his individual responsibility. (Anwar el-Sadat)

Like "duty," "law," "religion," the word "vocation" has a dull ring to it, but in terms of what it means, it is really not dull at all. *Vocare*, to call, of course, and man's vocation is a man's calling. It is the work that he is called to in this world, the thing that he is summoned to spend his life doing. We can speak of a man's choosing his vocation, but perhaps it is at least as accurate to speak of a vocation's choosing the man, of a call's being given and a man's hearing it, or not hearing it. And maybe that is the place to start: the business of listening and hearing. A man's life is full of all sorts of voices calling him in all sorts of directions. Some of them are voices from inside and some of them are voices from outside. The more alive and alert we are, the more clamorous our lives are. Which do we listen to? What kind of voice do we listen for? (Frederick Buechner)

II. Jesus' Way

Our parents are an inspiration to us as we look back on their lives of giving themselves for each other and for others. Had it not been for their lives of stewardship and giving, we would not perhaps have the faith we have today; and we want to pass that faith and love on to our children, grandchildren, and others. And then our thoughts are turned to the ultimate sacrifice that Christ made for us. He did so, not because he had to, but because of his great love for us. And to think, all he asks in return is for us to love him and others! But it would mean little to tell someone we love them if we did not try to show that love in a concrete way.

—Paul and Bettie Eck
Wichita, Kansas

THE EXAMPLE OF JESUS

Jesus is the supreme teacher of Christian stewardship, as he is of every other aspect of Christian life; and in Jesus' teaching and life self-emptying is fundamental. Now, it might seem that self-emptying has little to do with stewardship, but in Jesus' case that is not so. His self-emptying is not sterile self-denial for its own sake; rather, in setting aside self, he is filled with the Father's will, and he is fulfilled in just this way: "My food is to do the will of the one who sent me and to finish his work" (Jn 4:34).

Jesus' mission is to restore to good order the created household of God which sin has disrupted. He not only perfectly accomplishes this task, but also, in calling disciples, empowers them to collaborate with him in the work of redemption for themselves and on behalf of others.

In describing the resulting way of life, Jesus does not waste time proposing lofty but unrealistic ideals; he tells his followers how they are expected to live. The Beatitudes and the rest of the Sermon on the Mount prescribe the lifestyle of a Christian disciple (cf. Mt 5:3– 7:27). Although it does not suit worldly tastes, "the wisdom of this world is foolishness in the eyes of God" (1 Cor 3:19). One does well to live in this way. "Everyone who listens to these words of mine and acts on them will be like a wise man who built his house on a rock. . . . Everyone who listens to these words of mine but does not act on them will be like a fool who built his house on sand" (Mt 7:24, 26).

THE IMAGE OF THE STEWARD

Jesus sometimes describes a disciple's life in terms of stewardship (cf. Mt 25:14-30; Lk 12:42-48), not because being a steward is the whole of it but because this role sheds a certain light on it. An *oikonomos* or steward is one to whom the owner of a household turns over responsibility for caring for the property, managing affairs, making resources yield as much as possible, and sharing the resources with others. The position involves trust and accountability.

A parable near the end of Matthew's Gospel (cf. Mt 25:14-30) gives insight into Jesus' thinking about stewards and stewardship. It is the story of "a man who was going on a journey," and who left his wealth in silver pieces to be tended by three servants.

Two of them respond wisely by investing the money and making a handsome profit. Upon returning, the master commends them warmly and rewards them richly. But the third behaves foolishly, with anxious pettiness, squirreling away the master's wealth and earning nothing; he is rebuked and punished.

The silver pieces of this story stand for a great deal besides money. All temporal and spiritual goods are created by and come from God. That is true of everything human beings have: spiritual gifts like faith, hope, and love; talents of body and brain; cherished relationships with family and friends; material goods; the achievements of human genius and skill; the world itself. One day God will require an accounting of the use each person has made of the particular portion of these goods entrusted to him or her.

Each will be measured by the standard of his or her individual vocation. Each has received a different "sum"—a unique mix of talents, opportunities, challenges, weaknesses and strengths, potential modes of service and response—on which the Master expects a return. He will judge individuals according to what they have done with what they were given.

St. Ignatius of Loyola begins his *Spiritual Exercises* with a classic statement of the "first principle and foundation" permeating this way of life. "Human beings," he writes, "were created to praise, reverence and serve God our Lord, and by this means to save their souls. The other things on the face of the earth are created for them to help them in attaining the end for which they are created. Hence they are to make use of these things in as far as they help them in the attainment of their end, and they must rid themselves of them in as far as they provide a hindrance to them. . . . Our one desire and choice should be what is more conducive to the end for which we are created." St. Ignatius, fervently committed to the apostolate as he was, understood that the right use of things includes and requires that they be used to serve others.

What does all this say to busy people immersed in practical affairs? Is it advice only for those whose vocations lead them to withdraw from the world? Not as Jesus sees it: "But seek first the kingdom of God and his righteousness, and all these things will be given you besides" (Mt 6:33).

THE STEWARD'S REWARD

People trying to live as stewards reasonably wonder what reward they will receive. This is not selfishness but an expression of Christian hope. Peter raises the question when he says to Jesus, "We have given up everything and followed you" (Mk 10:28).

ALL TEMPORAL AND SPIRITUAL GOODS ARE CREATED BY AND COME FROM GOD.

Christ's response is more than Peter or any other disciple could reasonably hope or bargain for:

> There is no one who has given up house or brothers or sisters or mother or father or children or lands for my sake and for the sake of the gospel who will not receive a hundred times more now in this

> present age: houses and brothers and sisters and mothers and children and lands, with persecutions, and eternal life in the age to come. (Mk 10:29-30)

That is to say: Giving up means receiving more, including more responsibility as a steward; among the consequences of living this way will be persecution; and even though discipleship and stewardship set the necessary terms of Christian life in this world, they have their ultimate reward in another life.

Start, though, with the here and now. To be a Christian disciple is a rewarding way of life, a way of companionship with Jesus, and the practice of stewardship as a part of it is itself a source of deep joy. Those who live this way are happy people who have found the meaning and purpose of living.

For a long time religious believers—to say nothing of those who do not believe—have struggled with the question of what value to assign human activity. One solution is to consider it a means to an end: do good here and now for the sake of a reward in heaven. Another solution passes over the question of an afterlife: do good here and now for the sake of making this a better world.

Vatican Council II points to a third solution. It recognizes that human activity is valuable both for what it accomplishes here and now and also for its relationship to the hereafter. But, more important, it stresses not only the discontinuity between here and now and hereafter, but also the astonishing fact of continuity.

God's Kingdom already is present in history, imperfect but real (cf. Mt 10:7; *Lumen Gentium*, no. 48; *Gaudium et Spes*, no. 39). To be sure, it will come to fulfillment by God's power, on his terms, in his own good time. And yet, by their worthy deeds in this life, people also make a limited but real human contribution to building up the kingdom. They do so with an eye to present happiness and also to the perfect fulfillment which the Kingdom—and themselves as part of it—will enjoy in the life to come. The Council, therefore, teaches that the purpose of the human vocation to "earthly service" of one's fellow human beings is precisely to "make ready the material of the celestial realm" (*Gaudium et Spes*, no. 38).

In Christ, God has entered fully into human life and history. For one who is Christ's disciple there is no dichotomy, and surely no contradiction, between building the Kingdom and serving human purposes as a steward does. These are aspects of one and the same reality—the reality called the Christian life.

God's Kingdom is not an earthly kingdom, subject to decline and decay; it is the everlasting Kingdom of the life to come. But that "life to come" is in continuity with this present life through the human goods, the worthy human purposes, which people foster now. And after people have done their best, God will perfect human goods and bring about the final fulfillment of human persons. "The throne of God and of the Lamb will be in it, and his servants will worship him. They will look upon his face, and his name will be on their foreheads. Night will be no more, nor will they need light from lamp or sun, for the Lord God shall give them light, and they shall reign forever and ever" (Rev 22:3-5).

For Reflection and Discussion

1. What are the qualities in the life of Jesus that provide for us a standard by which to live? Make a list of these characteristics and evaluate your own life and the life of your community.

2. If you were preaching a sermon on stewardship, which one of Jesus' parables about stewardship would you emphasize the most?

3. What are the ways by which Jesus set an example of being a perfect steward?

4. What can a good steward realistically expect from God both in this life and in the life to come?

5. What should you do best in God's Kingdom on earth to prepare yourself for God's Kingdom in heaven?

6. What does the word of God say to you regarding the invitation and challenges in walking the way of Jesus?

    I am the vine, you are the branches. Those who remain in me and I in them will bear much fruit, because without me you can do nothing. (Jn 15:5)

    An argument arose among the disciples about which of them was the greatest. Jesus realized the intention of their hearts and took a child and placed it by his side and said to them, "Whoever receives this child in my name receives me, and whoever receives me receives the one who sent me. For the one who is least among all of you is the one who is the greatest." (Lk 9:46-48)

    Do not let your hearts be troubled. You have faith in God; have faith also in me. In my Father's house there are many dwelling places. If there were not, would I have told you that I am going to prepare a place for you? And if I go and prepare a place for you, I will come back again and take you to myself, so that where I am you also may be. (Jn 14:1-3)

7. Comment on the following passages:

> Being-with-Jesus refers to a manner of thinking, of acting, of loving, of relating to others, of viewing the world. It is a way of talking about our willingness to follow Jesus, to be drawn by his example, to learn from him, and to have our loyalties corrected and shaped by his. (William Reiser)

> The young creature in the stall of Bethlehem was a human being with human brain and heart and soul. And it was God. Its life was to manifest the will of the Father; to proclaim the sacred tidings, to stir mankind with the power of God, to establish the Covenant, and shoulder the sin of the world, expiating it with love and leading mankind through the destruction of sacrifice and the victory of the Resurrection into the new existence of grace. In this accomplishment alone lay Jesus' self-perfection: fulfillment of mission and personal fulfillment were one. (Romano Guardini)

> Christians, on pilgrimage toward the heavenly city, should seek and savor the things which are above. This duty in no way decreases, but rather increases, the weight of their obligation to work with all men in constructing a more human world. In fact, the mystery of the Christian faith furnishes them with excellent incentives and helps toward discharging this duty more energetically and especially toward uncovering the full meaning of this activity, a meaning which gives human culture its eminent place in the integral vocation of man. (*Gaudium et Spes*, no. 57)

III. Living as a Steward

I have learned to share because I want to, not because I need to. There are no controls, no strings attached, and no guarantee when we give unconditionally. That doesn't mean that in retrospect I haven't questioned my decisions; it simply means that I've tried to look at it as a growth experience, always keeping in mind the life of Jesus Christ. I personally see stewardship as a nurturing process. It is, in a sense, an invitation to reassess our priorities. It is ongoing and often painful, but most of all it brings a personal sense of happiness and peace of mind as I continue my journey through life.

—Jim Hogan
Green Bay, Wisconsin

CREATION AND STEWARDSHIP

Although it would be a mistake to think that stewardship by itself includes the whole of Christian life, in probing the Christian meaning of stewardship one confronts an astonishing fact: God wishes human beings to be his collaborators in the work of creation, redemption, and sanctification; and such collaboration involves stewardship in its most profound sense. We exercise such stewardship, furthermore, not merely by our own power but by the power of the Spirit of truth, whom Jesus promises to his followers (cf. Jn 14:16-17), and whom we see at work at the first Pentecost inspiring the apostles to commence that proclamation of the good news which has continued to this day (cf. Acts 2:1-4).

The great story told in Scripture, the story of God's love for humankind, begins with God at work as Creator, maker of all that is: "In the beginning, when God created the heavens and the earth . . ." (Gn 1:1). Among God's creatures are human persons: "The Lord God formed man out of the clay of the ground and blew into his nostrils the breath of life" (Gn 2:7). God not only creates human beings, however, but also bestows on them the divine image and likeness (cf. Gn 1:26). As part of this resemblance to God, people are called to cooperate with the Creator in continuing the divine work (cf. Pope John Paul II, *Laborem Exercens*, no. 25).

Stewardship of creation is one expression of this. The divine mandate to our first parents makes that clear. "Be fertile and multiply; fill the earth and subdue it. Have dominion over the fish of the sea, the birds of the air, and all the living things that move on the earth" (Gn 1:28). Subduing and exercising dominion do not mean abusing the earth. Rather, as the second creation story explains, God settled humankind upon earth to be its steward—"to cultivate and care for it" (Gn 2:15).

This human activity of cultivating and caring has a generic name: work. It is not a punishment for or a consequence of sin. True, sin does painfully skew the experience of work: "By the sweat of your face shall you get bread to eat" (Gn 3:19). But, even so, God's mandate to humankind to collaborate with him in the task of creating—the command to work—comes *before* the Fall. Work is a fundamental aspect of the human vocation. It is necessary for human happiness and fulfillment. It is intrinsic to responsible stewardship of the world.

So, as Vatican II observes, far from imagining that the products of human effort are "in opposition to God's power, and that the rational creature exists as a kind of rival to the Creator," Christians see human achievements as "a sign of God's greatness and the flowering of his own mysterious design" (*Gaudium et Spes*, no. 34). While it is lived out by individual women and men in countless ways corresponding to their personal vocations, human cooperation with God's work of creation in general takes several forms.

COLLABORATORS IN CREATION

One of these is a profound reverence for the great gift of life, their own lives and the lives of others, along with readiness to spend themselves in serving all that preserves and enhances life.

ECOLOGICAL STEWARDSHIP MEANS CULTIVATING A HEIGHTENED SENSE OF HUMAN INTERDEPENDENCE AND SOLIDARITY.

This reverence and readiness begin with opening one's eyes to how precious a gift life really is—and that is not easy, in view of our tendency to take the gift for granted. "Do any human beings ever realize life while they live it?—every, every minute?" demands Emily in *Our Town*. And the Stage Manager replies, "No. The saints and poets, maybe—they do some" (Thornton Wilder, *Our Town* [New York: Harper and Row, 1958], 100). Yet it is necessary to make the effort. For Vatican II speaks of the "surpassing ministry of safeguarding life" and declares that "from the moment of its conception life must be guarded with the greatest care" (*Gaudium et Spes*, no. 51).

Partly too, stewardship of the world is expressed by jubilant appreciation of nature, whose God-given beauty not even exploitation and abuse have destroyed.

> And for all this, nature is never spent;
> There lives the dearest freshness deep down
> things
> And though the last lights off the black West
> went
> Oh, morning, at the brown brink east-
> ward springs—
> Because the Holy Ghost over the bent
> World broods with warm breast and with
> ah! bright wings.

(Gerard Manley Hopkins, "God's Grandeur," in *Poems of Gerard Manley Hopkins* [New York, Oxford University Press, 1950], 70)

Beyond simply appreciating natural beauty, there is the active stewardship of ecological concern. Ecological stewardship means cultivating a heightened sense of human interdependence and solidarity. It therefore calls for renewed efforts to address what Pope John Paul II calls "the structural forms of poverty" existing in this country and on the international level (*Message for the World Day of Peace*, January 1, 1990). And it underlines the need to reduce military spending and do away with war and weapons of war.

Especially this form of stewardship requires that many people adopt simpler lifestyles. This is true, not only of affluent persons and societies, but also of those who may not be affluent as that term is commonly understood yet do enjoy access to superfluous material goods and comforts. Within the Church, for example, it is important to avoid even the appearance of consumerism and luxury, and this obligation begins with us bishops. As Pope John Paul II says, "simplicity, moderation, and discipline, as well as a spirit of sacrifice, must become a part of everyday life, lest all suffer the negative consequences of the careless habits of a few" (ibid.).

At the same time, life as a Christian steward also requires continued involvement in the human vocation to cultivate material creation. This productivity embraces art, scholarship, science, and technology, as well as business and trade, physical labor, skilled work of all kinds, and serving others. So-called ordinary work offers at least as many opportunities as do supposedly more glamorous occupations. A woman who works at a supermarket checkout counter writes: "I feel that my job consists of a lot more than ringing up orders, taking people's money, and bagging their groceries. . . . By doing my job well I know I have a chance to do God's work too. Because of this, I try to make each of my customers feel special. While I'm serving them, they become the most important people in my life" (Maxine F. Dennis, in *Of Human Hands* [Minneapolis and Chicago: Augsburg Fortress/ACTA Publications, 1991], 49).

REDEMPTION AND STEWARDSHIP

Everyone has some natural responsibility for a portion of the world and an obligation in caring for it to acknowledge God's dominion. But there are also those who might be called stewards by grace. Baptism makes Christians stewards of this kind, able to act explicitly on God's behalf in cultivating and serving the portion of the world entrusted to their care. We find the perfect model of such stewardship in the Lord. "For in him all the fullness was pleased to dwell, and through him to reconcile all things for him, making peace by the blood of his cross" (Col 1:19-20); and finally it will be he who "hands over the kingdom to his God and Father" (1 Cor 15:24).

Although Jesus is the unique priest and mediator, his disciples share in his priestly work. Baptism makes them "a royal priesthood" (1 Pt 2:9) called to offer up the world and all that is in it—especially themselves—to the Lord of all. In exercising this office, they most fully realize the meaning of our Christian stewardship. Part of what is involved here for Catholics is a stewardship of time, which should include setting aside periods for family prayer, for the reading of Scripture, for visits to the Blessed Sacrament, and for attendance at Mass during the week whenever this is possible.

Participation in Christ's redemptive activity extends even, though certainly not only, to the use people make of experiences that otherwise might seem the least promising: deprivation, loss, pain. "Now I rejoice in my sufferings for your sake," St. Paul says, "and in my flesh I am filling up what is lacking in the afflictions of Christ on behalf of his body, which is the church" (Col 1:24). Here also one looks to Jesus to lead the way. For one's estimate of suffering, as Pope John Paul II points out, is transformed by discovering its "salvific meaning" when united with the suffering of Christ (*Salvifici Doloris*, no. 27).

COOPERATION IN REDEMPTION

Penance also belongs to this aspect of Christian life. Today as in the past, the Church commends what Pope Paul VI called the "traditional triad" of prayer, fasting, and almsgiving (*Paenitemini*, February 17, 1966), while also encouraging Catholics to adopt penitential practices of their own choice that suit their particular circumstances.

Through voluntarily accepted penance one gradually becomes liberated from those obstacles to Christian discipleship which a secularized culture exalting individual gratification places in one's way. These obstacles include not just the quest for pleasure but also avarice, a craving for the illusion of absolute dominion and control, valuing creatures without reference to their Creator, excessive individualism, and ultimately the fear of death unrelieved by hope for eternal life. These are consequences of sin—sin which threatens the way of life of Christian stewardship and the identity of Christians as disciples of the Lord. "Let us master this great and simple truth," Cardinal Newman once said, "that all rich materials and productions of this world, being God's property, are intended for God's service; and sin only, nothing but sin, turns them to a different purpose" ("Offerings for the Sanctuary" in *Parochial and Plain Sermons* [San Francisco: Ignatius Press, 1987], 1368).

Sin causes people to turn in on themselves; to become grasping and exploitative toward possessions and other people; to grow accustomed to conducting relationships not by the standards of generous stewardship but by the calculus of self-interest: "What's in it for me?" Constantly, Christians must beg God for the grace of conversion: the grace to know who they are, to whom they belong, how they are to live—the grace to repent and change and grow, the grace to become good disciples and stewards.

But if they do accept God's grace and, repenting, struggle to change, God will respond like the father of the Prodigal Son. "Filled with compassion" at seeing his repentant child approaching after a long and painful separation, this loving parent "ran to his son, embraced him and kissed him" even before the boy could stammer out the words of sorrow he had rehearsed (Lk 15:20). God's love is always there. The Spirit of wisdom and courage helps people seek pardon and be mindful, in the face of all their forgetting, that the most important work of their lives is to be Jesus' disciples.

Thus, the stewardship of disciples is not reducible only to one task or another. It involves embracing, cultivating, enjoying, sharing—and sometimes also giving up—the goods of human life. Christians live this way in the confidence that comes from faith: for they know that the human goods they cherish and cultivate will be perfected—and they themselves will be fulfilled—in that Kingdom, already present, which Christ will bring to perfection and one day hand over to the Father.

For Reflection and Discussion

1. If you were to undertake stewardship as a way of Christian life, what major problems and pain would you anticipate?

2. In your lifetime, how have you experienced co-creation with God?

3. How do you relate Christian stewardship to ecology, to your personal care for the environment?

4. How do you react to the idea of "being our brother's keeper," of being involved in efforts to curtail consumerism so that God's good things will benefit not only some but all people?

5. Do you see the theological connection between stewardship and "priestly mediation"?

6. What does the word of God say to you regarding the life of stewardship?

> You are the salt of the earth. But if salt loses its taste, with what can it be seasoned? It is no longer good for anything but to be thrown out and trampled underfoot. You are the light of the world. A city set on a mountain cannot be hidden. Nor do they light a lamp and then put it under a bushel basket; it is set on a lampstand, where it gives light to all in the house. Just so, your light must shine before others, that they may see your good deeds and glorify your heavenly Father. (Mt 5:13-16)
>
> There are different kinds of spiritual gifts but the same Spirit; there are different forms of service but the same Lord; there are different workings but the same God who produces all of them in everyone. (1 Cor 12:4-6)
>
> It was not you who chose me, but I who chose you and appointed you to go and bear fruit that will remain, so that whatever you ask the Father in my name he may give you. This I command you: love one another. (Jn 15:16-17)

7. Comment on the following passages:

> Whence it is, that if Christians are also joined in mind and heart with the most Holy Redeemer, when they apply themselves to temporal affairs, their work in a way is a continuation of the labor of Jesus Christ Himself, drawing from it strength and redemptive power: "He who abides in Me, and I in him, he bears much fruit." Human labor of this kind is so exalted and ennobled that it leads men engaged in it to spiritual perfection and can likewise contribute to the diffusion and propagation of the fruits of the Redemption to others. (Pope John XXIII, *Mater et Magistra*, no. 259)

> In the sense of a "job," work is a way of making money and making a living. It supports a self defined by economic success, security, and all that money can buy. In the sense of a "career," work traces one's progress through life by achievement and advancement in an occupation. It yields a self defined by a broader sort of success, which takes in social standing and prestige, and by a sense of expanding power and competency that renders work itself a source of self-esteem. In the strongest sense of a "calling," work constitutes a practical idea of activity and character that makes a person's work morally inseparable from his or her life. It subsumes the self into a community of disciplined practice and sound judgment whose activity has meaning and value in itself not just in the output or profit that results from it. But the calling not only links a person to his or her fellow workers, a calling links a person to the larger community, a whole in which the calling of each is a contribution to the good of all. (Robert Bellah)

> Unfortunately, certain types of Christian piety intensify this problem of putting so much emphasis on the life of heaven that human activity on this earth is devalued. Teilhard [de Chardin] thought that about 90 percent of the practicing Christians of his time looked upon their work as "spiritual encumbrance" which took them away from a close relationship to God. He sensed the great conflict in the hearts of many believers who live double lives because they cannot reconcile their faith in God with their care for the world. They are not able to find real organic connections between their worship on Sunday and their work during the week. In Teilhard's view the traditional solution of sanctifying one's daily efforts through prayer and good intention is helpful but incomplete, because it still considers daily work as insignificant in itself and detrimental to the spiritual life. (James Bacik)

IV. Stewards of the Church

When I began to provide dental treatment for persons with AIDS, I knew HIV-positive people desperately needed this service, but I did not know how much I needed them. Time and again, reaching out to serve and heal, I have found myself served and healed. Their courage, compassion, wisdom, and faith have changed my life. I have faced my own mortality, and I rejoice in the daily gift of life. My love for people has taken on new dimensions. I hug and kiss my wife and family more than ever and see them as beautiful gifts from God. My ministry as a deacon has become dynamic, and I regard my profession as a vital part of it.

—*Dr. Anthony M. Giambalvo*
Rockville Centre, New York

COMMUNITY AND STEWARDSHIP

The New Covenant in and through Christ—the reconciliation he effects between humankind and God—forms a community: the new People of God, the Body of Christ, the Church. The unity of this people is itself a precious good, to be cherished, preserved, and built up by lives of love. The epistle to the Ephesians exhorts Christians to "live in a manner worthy of the call you have received, with all humility and gentleness, with patience, bearing with one another through love, striving to preserve the unity of the spirit through the bond of peace: one body and one Spirit, as you were also called to the one hope of your call; one Lord, one faith, one baptism; one God and Father of all" (Eph 4:1-6).

Because its individual members do collectively make up the Body of Christ, that body's health and well-being are the responsibility of the members—the personal responsibility of each one of us. We all are stewards of the Church. As "to each individual the manifestation of the Spirit is given for some benefit" (1 Cor 12:7), so stewardship in an ecclesial setting means cherishing and fostering the gifts of all, while using one's own gifts to serve the community of faith. The rich tradition of tithing set forth in the Old Testament is an expression of this. (See, for example, Dt 14:22; Lv 27:30.) Those who set their hearts upon spiritual gifts must "seek to have an abundance for building up the church" (1 Cor 14:12).

But how is the Church built up? In a sense there are as many answers to that question as there are individual members with individual vocations. But the overarching answer for all is this: through personal participation in and support of the Church's mission of proclaiming and teaching, serving and sanctifying.

This participation takes different forms according to people's different gifts and offices, but there is a fundamental obligation arising from the sacrament of Baptism (cf. Pope John Paul II, *Christifideles*

Laici, no. 15): that people place their gifts, their resources—their selves—at God's service in and through the Church. Here also Jesus is the model. Even though his perfect self-emptying is unique, it is within the power of disciples, and a duty, that they be generous stewards of the Church, giving freely of their time, talent, and treasure. "Consider this," Paul says, addressing not only the Christians of Corinth but all of us. "Whoever sows sparingly will also reap sparingly, and whoever sows bountifully will also reap bountifully. . . . God loves a cheerful giver" (2 Cor 9:6-7).

EVANGELIZATION AND STEWARDSHIP

In various ways, then, stewardship of the Church leads people to share in the work of evangelization or proclaiming the Good News, in the work of catechesis or transmitting and strengthening the faith, and in works of justice and mercy on behalf of persons in need. Stewardship requires support for the Church's institutions and programs for these purposes. But, according to their opportunities and circumstances, members of the Church also should engage in such activities personally and on their own initiative.

Parents, for instance, have work of great importance to do in the domestic church, the home. Within the family, they must teach their children the truths of the faith and pray with them; share Christian values with them in the face of pressures to conform to the hostile values of a secularized society; and initiate them into the practice of stewardship itself, in all its dimensions, contrary to today's widespread consumerism and individualism. This may require adjusting the family's own patterns of consumption and its lifestyle, including the use of television and other media which sometimes preach values in conflict with the mind of Christ. Above all, it requires that parents themselves be models of stewardship, especially by their selfless service to one another, to their children, and to church and community needs.

Parishes, too, must be, or become, true communities of faith within which this Christian way of life is learned and practiced. Sound business practice is a fundamental of good stewardship, and stewardship as it relates to church finances must include the most stringent ethical, legal, and fiscal standards. That requires several things: pastors and parish staff must be open, consultative, collegial, and accountable in the conduct of affairs. And parishioners must accept responsibility for their parishes and contribute generously—both money and personal service—to their programs and projects. The success or failure of parish programs, the vitality of parish life or its absence, the ability or inability of a parish to render needed services to its members and the community depend upon all.

PARENTS HAVE WORK OF GREAT IMPORTANCE TO DO IN THE DOMESTIC CHURCH, THE HOME.

We, therefore, urge the Catholics of every parish in our land to ponder the words of St. Paul: "Now as you excel in every respect, in faith, discourse, knowledge, all earnestness, and in the love we have for you, may you excel in this gracious act also" (2 Cor 8:7). Only by living as generous stewards of these local Christian communities, their parishes, can the Catholics of the United States hope to make them the vital sources of faith-filled Christian dynamism they are meant to be.

At the same time, stewardship in and for the parish should not be narrowly parochial. For the diocese is not merely an administrative structure but instead joins communities called parishes into a "local church" and unites its people in faith, worship, and service. The same spirit of personal responsibility in which a Catholic approaches his or her parish should extend to the diocese and be expressed in essentially the same ways: generous material support and self-giving. As in the case of the parish, too, lay Catholics ought to have an active role in the oversight of the stewardship of pastoral leaders and administrators at the diocesan level. At the present time, it seems clear that many Catholics need to develop a better understanding of the financial needs of the Church at the diocesan level. Indeed, the spirit and practice of stewardship should extend to other local churches and to the universal Church—to the Christian community and to one's sisters and brothers in Christ everywhere—and be expressed in deeds of service and mutual support. For some, this will mean direct personal participation in evangelization and mission work, for others generous giving to the collections established for these purposes and other worthy programs.

Every member of the Church is called to evangelize, and the practice of authentic Christian stewardship inevitably leads to evangelization. As stewards of the mysteries of God (cf. 1 Cor 4:1), people desire to tell others about them and about the light they shed on human life, to share the gifts and graces they have received from God, especially knowledge of Christ Jesus, "who became for us wisdom from God, as well as righteousness, sanctification, and redemption" (1 Cor 1:30). Human beings, says Pope Paul VI, "have the right to know the riches of the mystery of Christ. It is in these . . . that the whole human family can find in the most comprehensive form and beyond all their expectations everything for which they have been groping" (*Evangelii Nuntiandi*, no. 53).

SOLIDARITY AND STEWARDSHIP

While the unity arising from the covenant assumes and requires human solidarity, it also goes beyond it, producing spiritual fruit insofar as it is founded on union with the Lord. "I am the vine, you are the branches," Jesus says. "Whoever remains in me and I in him will bear much fruit" (Jn 15:5). As Simone Weil remarks, "A single piece of bread given to a hungry man is enough to save a soul—if it is given in the right way."

In this world, however, solidarity encounters many obstacles on both the individual and social levels. It is essential that Jesus' disciples do what can be done to remove them.

The most basic and pervasive obstacle is sheer selfish lack of love, a lack which people must acknowledge and seek to correct when they find it in their own hearts and lives. For the absence of charity from the lives of disciples of Jesus in itself is self-defeating and hypocritical. "If anyone says, 'I love God,' but hates his brother, he is a liar" (1 Jn 4:20).

Extreme disparities in wealth and power also block unity and communion. Such disparities exist today between person and person, social class and social class, nation and nation. They are contrary to that virtue of solidarity, grounded in charity, which Pope John Paul II commends as the basis of a world order embodying "a new model of the unity of the human race" whose "supreme model" is the intimate life of the Trinity itself (*Sollicitudo Rei Socialis*, no. 40). Familiarity with the Church's growing body of social doctrine is necessary in order to grasp and respond to the practical requirements of discipleship and stewardship in light of the complex realities of today's national and international socioeconomic life.

Social justice, which the pastoral letter *Economic Justice for All* calls a kind of contributive justice, is a particular aspect of the virtue of solidarity. Encompassing the duty of "all who are able to create the goods, services, and other nonmaterial or spiritual values necessary for the welfare of the whole community," it gives moral as well as economic content to the concept of productivity. Thus productivity "cannot be measured solely by its output of goods and services." Rather, "patterns of productivity must . . . be measured in light of their impact on the fulfillment of basic needs, employment levels, patterns of discrimination, environmental impact, and sense of community" (*Economic Justice for All*, no. 71).

Finally, and most poignantly, solidarity is obstructed by the persistence of religious conflicts and divisions, including those that sunder even followers of Christ. Christians remain tragically far from realizing Jesus' priestly prayer "that they may all be one, as you, Father, are in me and I in you" (Jn 17:21).

As all this suggests, our individual lives as disciples and stewards must be seen in relation to God's larger purposes. From the outset of his covenanting, God had it in mind to make many one. He promised Abram: "I will make of you a great nation, and I will bless you; I will make your name great, so that you will be a blessing. . . . All the communities of the earth shall find blessing in you" (Gn 12:23). In Jesus, the Kingdom of God is inaugurated—a kingdom open to all. Those who enter into Jesus' New Covenant find themselves growing in a union of minds and hearts with others who also have responded to God's call. They find their hearts and minds expanding to embrace all men and women, especially those in need, in a communion of mercy and love.

EUCHARISTIC STEWARDSHIP

The Eucharist is the great sign and agent of this expansive communion of charity. "Because the loaf of bread is one, we, though many, are one body, for we all partake of the one loaf" (1 Cor 10:17). Here people enjoy a unique union with Christ and, in him, with one another. Here his love—indeed, his very self—flows into his disciples and, through them and their practice of stewardship, to the entire human race. Here Jesus renews his covenant-forming act of perfect fidelity to God, while also making it possible for us to cooperate. In the Eucharist, Christians reaffirm their participation in the New Covenant; they give thanks to God for blessings received; and they strengthen their bonds of commitment to one another as members of the covenant community Jesus forms.

And what do Christians bring to the Eucharistic celebration and join there with Jesus' offering? Their lives as Christian disciples; their personal vocations and the stewardship they have exercised regarding them; their individual contributions to the great work of restoring all things in Christ. Disciples give thanks to God for gifts received and strive to share them with others. That is why, as Vatican II says of the Eucharist, "if this celebration is to be sincere and thorough, it must lead to various works of charity and mutual help, as well as to missionary activity and to different forms of Christian witness" (*Presbyterorum Ordinis*, no. 6).

More than that, the Eucharist is the sign and agent of that heavenly communion in which we shall together share, enjoying the fruits of stewardship "freed of stain, burnished and transfigured" (*Gaudium et Spes*, no. 39). It is not only the promise but the commencement of the heavenly banquet where human lives are perfectly fulfilled.

We have Jesus' word for it: "Whoever eats this bread will live forever; and the bread that I will give is my flesh for the life of the world" (Jn 6:51). The glory and the boast of Christian stewards lie in mirroring, however poorly, the stewardship of Jesus Christ, who gave and still gives all he has and is, in order to be faithful to God's will and carry through to completion his redemptive stewardship of human beings and their world.

For Reflection and Discussion

1. Have you, like Dr. Giambalvo, had the experience of being "served and healed" by those you set out to serve and heal?

2. What are the implications of God's calling us into a love relationship (covenant) and of being a people uniquely his own? What does this say about dignity, equality, unity?

3. How would you go about connecting the Eucharist with your practice of stewardship?

4. Within the institutional Church, of which you are a member, what, in order of priority, are your stewardship responsibilities?

5. Is there more to "stewardship within the Church" than donations of "time, talent, and treasure"?

6. How will "Eucharistic stewardship" develop your convictions about global solidarity—"the world is God's village on earth"?

7. What does the word of God say to you about covenant, community, solidarity—about being Eucharistic stewards?

> [Jesus] asked them, "How many loaves do you have?" "Seven," they replied. He ordered the crowd to sit down on the ground. Then, taking the seven loaves he gave thanks, broke them, and gave them to his disciples to distribute, and they distributed them to the crowd. They also had a few fish. He said the blessing over them and ordered them distributed also. They ate and were satisfied. They picked up the fragments left over—seven baskets. (Mk 8:5-8)
>
> According to the grace of God given to me, like a wise master builder I laid a foundation, and another is building upon it. But each one must be careful how he builds upon it, for no one can lay a foundation other than the one that is there, namely, Jesus Christ. If anyone builds on this foundation with gold, silver, precious stones, wood, hay, or straw, the work of each will come to light, for the Day will disclose it. It will be revealed

with fire, and the fire [itself] will test the quality of each one's work. (1 Cor 3:10-13)

For I will take you away from among the nations, gather you from all the foreign lands, and bring you back to your own land. I will sprinkle clean water upon you to cleanse you from all your impurities, and from all your idols I will cleanse you. I will give you a new heart and place a new spirit within you, taking from your bodies your stony hearts and giving you natural hearts. I will put my spirit within you and make you live by my statutes, careful to observe my decrees. You shall live in the land I gave your fathers; you shall be my people, and I will be your God. (Ez 36:24-28)

8. Comment on the following passages:

A community is a group of persons who share a history and whose common set of interpretations about that history provide the basis for common actions. These interpretations may be quite diverse and controversial even within the community, but are sufficient to provide the individual members with the sense that they are more alike than unlike. (Stanley Hauerwas)

[A correct understanding of the common good] embraces the sum total of all those conditions of social living, whereby men are enabled more fully and more readily to achieve their own perfection. (Pope John XXIII, *Mater et Magistra*)

God's kingdom therefore is no fixed, existing order, but a living, nearing thing. Long remote, it now advances, little by little, and has come so close as to demand acceptance. Kingdom of God means a state in which God is king and consequently rules. (Romano Guardini)

V. The Christian Steward

It was sixteen years ago, but it seems like only yesterday. I was suddenly confronted with serious surgery, which I never thought would happen to me. It always happened to others. The memory is still there, and I recall vividly the days before the surgery. I really received the grace to ask myself, "What do I own, and what owns me?" When you are wheeled into a surgery room, it really doesn't matter who you are or what you possess. What counts is the confidence in a competent surgical staff and a good and gracious God. I know that my whole understanding and appreciation of the gifts and resources I possess took on new meaning. It is amazing how a divine economy of life and health provides a unique perspective of what really matters.

—Most Reverend Thomas J. Murphy
Archbishop of Seattle

While the New Testament does not provide a rounded portrait of the Christian steward all in one place, elements of such a portrait are present throughout its pages.

In the Gospel, Jesus speaks of the "faithful and prudent steward" as one whom a householder sets over other members of the household in order to "distribute the food allowance at the proper time" (Lk 12:42; cf. Mt 24:25). Evidently, good stewards understand that they are to share with others what they have received, that this must be done in a timely way, and that God will hold them accountable for how well or badly they do it.

For if a steward wastes the owner's goods and mistreats the other household members, "that servant's master will come on an unexpected day and at an unknown hour and will punish him severely and assign him a place with the unfaithful" (Lk 12:46).

In the lives of disciples, however, something else must come before the practice of stewardship. They need a flash of insight—a certain way of *seeing*—by which they view the world and their relationship to it in a fresh, new light. "The world is charged with the grandeur of God," Gerard Manley Hopkins exclaims; more than anything else, it may be this glimpse of the divine grandeur in all that is that sets people on the path of Christian stewardship.

Not only in material creation do people discern God present and active, but also, and especially, in the human heart.

"Do not be deceived . . . all good giving and every perfect gift is from above" (Jas 1:16-17), and this is true above all where spiritual gifts are concerned. Various as they are, "one and the same Spirit produces all of these" (1 Cor 12:11)—including the gift of discernment itself, which leads men and women to say: "We have not received the spirit of the world but the Spirit that is from God, so that we may understand the things freely given us by God" (1 Cor 2:12). So it is that people have the power to live as stewards, striving to realize the ideal set forth by Paul: "Whether you eat or drink, or whatever you do, do everything for the glory of God" (1 Cor 10:31).

Christian stewards are conscientious and faithful. After all, the first requirement of a steward is to be "found trustworthy" (1 Cor 4:2). In the present case, moreover, stewardship is a uniquely solemn trust. If Christians understand it and strive to live it to the full, they grasp the fact that they are no less than "God's co-workers" (1 Cor 3:9), with their own particular share in his creative, redemptive, and sanctifying work. In this light, stewards are fully conscious of their accountability. They neither live nor die as their own masters; rather, "if we live, we live for the Lord, and if we die, we die for the Lord; so then, whether we live or die, we are the Lord's" (Rom 14:8).

THE LIFE OF A CHRISTIAN STEWARD, LIVED IN IMITATION OF THE LIFE OF CHRIST, IS CHALLENGING, EVEN DIFFICULT IN MANY WAYS; BUT BOTH HERE AND HEREAFTER IT IS CHARGED WITH INTENSE JOY.

Christian stewards are generous out of love as well as duty. They dare not fail in charity and what it entails, and the New Testament is filled with warnings to those who might be tempted to substitute some counterfeit for authentic love. For example: "If someone who has worldly means sees a brother in need and refuses him compassion, how can the love of God remain in him?" (1 Jn 3:17). Or this: "Come now, you rich, weep and wail over your impending miseries. Your wealth has rotted away, your clothes have become moth-eaten, your gold and silver have corroded, and that corrosion will be a testimony against you; it will devour your flesh like a fire. You have stored up treasure for the last days" (Jas 5:1-3).

What, then, are Christians to do? Of course people's lives as stewards take countless forms, according to their unique vocations and circumstances. Still, the fundamental pattern in every case is simple and changeless: "Serve one another through love . . . bear one another's burdens, and so you will fulfill the law of Christ" (Gal 5:13, 6:2). This includes being stewards of the Church, for, as we are quite specifically told, "the Church of the living God" is "the household of God" (1 Tim 3:15), and it is essential to practice stewardship there.

The life of a Christian steward, lived in imitation of the life of Christ, is challenging, even difficult in many ways; but both here and hereafter it is charged with intense joy. Like Paul, the good steward is able to say, "I am filled with encouragement, I am overflowing with joy all the more because of all our affliction" (2 Cor 7:4). Women and men who seek to live in this way learn that "all things work for good for those who love God" (Rom 8:28). It is part of their personal experience that God is "rich in mercy [and] we are his handiwork, created in Christ Jesus for the good works that God has prepared in advance, that we should live in them" (Eph 2:4, 10). They readily cry out from the heart: "Rejoice in the Lord always! I shall say it again: Rejoice!" (Phil 4:4). They look forward in hope to hearing the Master's words addressed to those who have lived as disciples faithful in their practice of stewardship should: "Come, you who are blessed by my Father. Inherit the kingdom prepared for you from the foundation of the world" (Mt 25:34).

After Jesus, it is the Blessed Virgin Mary who by her example most perfectly teaches the meaning of discipleship and stewardship in their fullest sense. All of their essential elements are found in her life: she was called and gifted by God; she responded generously, creatively, and prudently; she understood her divinely assigned role as "handmaid" in terms of service and fidelity (see Lk 1:26-56).

As Mother of God, her stewardship consisted of her maternal service and devotion to Jesus, from infancy to adulthood, up to the agonizing hours of Jesus' death (Jn 19:25). As Mother of the Church, her stewardship is clearly articulated in the closing chapter of the Second Vatican Council's *Constitution on the Church, Lumen Gentium* (cf. nos. 52-69). Pope John Paul II observes: "Mary is one of the first who 'believed,' and precisely with her faith as Spouse and Mother she wishes to act upon all those who entrust themselves to her as children" (*Redemptoris Mater*, no. 46).

In light of all this, it only remains for all of us to ask ourselves this question: Do we also wish to be disciples of Jesus Christ? The Spirit is ready to show us the way—a way of which stewardship is a part.

Genesis, telling the story of creation, says God looked upon what had been made and found it good; and seeing the world's goodness, God entrusted it to human beings. "The Lord God planted a garden" and placed there human persons "to cultivate and care for it" (Gn 2:8, 15). Now, as then and always, it is a central part of the human vocation that we be good stewards of what we have received—this garden, this divine human workshop, this world and all that is in it—setting minds and hearts and hands to the task of creating and redeeming in cooperation with our God, Creator and Lord of all.

Appendix I

To Be a Christian Steward

A Summary of the U.S. Bishops' Pastoral Letter on Stewardship

"As each one has received a gift, use it to serve one another as good stewards of God's varied grace" (1 Pt 4:10).

What identifies a steward? Safeguarding material and human resources and using them responsibly are one answer; so is generous giving of time, talent, and treasure. But being a Christian steward means more. As Christian stewards, we receive God's gifts gratefully, cultivate them responsibly, share them lovingly in justice with others, and return them with increase to the Lord.

DISCIPLES AS STEWARDS

Let us begin with being a disciple—a follower of our Lord Jesus Christ. As members of the Church, Jesus calls us to be disciples. This has astonishing implications:

- Mature disciples make a conscious decision to follow Jesus, no matter what the cost.
- Christian disciples experience conversion—life-shaping changes of mind and heart—and commit their very selves to the Lord.
- Christian stewards respond in a particular way to the call to be a disciple. Stewardship has the power to shape and mold our understanding of our lives and the way in which we live.

Jesus' disciples and Christian stewards recognize God as the origin of life, giver of freedom, and source of all things. We are grateful for the gifts we have received and are eager to use them to show our love for God and for one another. We look to the life and teaching of Jesus for guidance in living as Christian stewards.

STEWARDS OF CREATION

The Bible contains a profound message about the stewardship of material creation: God created the world, but entrusts it to human beings. Caring for and cultivating the world involves the following:

- Joyful appreciation for the God-given beauty and wonder of nature;
- Protection and preservation of the environment, which would be the stewardship of ecological concern;
- Respect for human life—shielding life from threat and assault, doing everything that can be done to enhance this gift and make life

flourish; and

- Development of this world through noble human effort—physical labor, the trades and professions, the arts and sciences. We call such effort "work."

Work is a fulfilling human vocation. The Second Vatican Council points out that, through work, we build up not only our world but the Kingdom of God, already present among us. Work is a partnership with God—our share in a divine human collaboration in creation. It occupies a central place in our lives as Christian stewards.

STEWARDS OF VOCATION

Jesus calls us, as his disciples, to a new way of life—the Christian way of life—of which stewardship is part. But Jesus does not call us as nameless people in a faceless crowd. He calls us individually, by name. Each one of us—clergy, religious, lay person; married, single; adult, child—has a personal vocation. God intends each one of us to play a unique role in carrying out the divine plan.

The challenge, then, is to understand our role—our vocation—and to respond generously to this call from God. Christian vocation entails the practice of stewardship. In addition, Christ calls each of us to be stewards of our personal vocations, which we receive from God.

STEWARDS OF THE CHURCH

Stewards of God's gifts are not passive beneficiaries. We cooperate with God in our own redemption and in the redemption of others.

We are also obliged to be stewards of the Church—collaborators and cooperators in continuing the redemptive work of Jesus Christ, which is the Church's essential mission. This mission—proclaiming and teaching, serving and sanctifying—is our task. It is the personal responsibility of each one of us as stewards of the Church.

All members of the Church have their own roles to play in carrying out its mission:

- Parents, who nurture their children in the light of faith;

- Parishioners, who work in concrete ways to make their parishes true communities of faith and vibrant sources of service to the larger community;

- All Catholics, who give generous support—time, money, prayers, and personal service according to their circumstances—to parish and diocesan programs and to the universal Church.

OBSTACLES TO STEWARDSHIP

People who want to live as Christian disciples and Christian stewards face serious obstacles.

In the United States and other nations, a dominant secular culture often contradicts religious convictions about the meaning of life. This culture frequently encourages us to focus on ourselves and our pleasures. At times, we can find it far too easy to ignore spiritual realities and to deny religion a role in shaping human and social values.

As Catholics who have entered into the mainstream of American society and experienced its advantages, many of us also have been adversely influenced by this secular culture. We know what it is to struggle against selfishness and greed, and we realize that it is harder for many today to accept the challenge of being a Christian steward.

It is essential, therefore, that we make a special effort to understand the true meaning of stewardship and live accordingly.

A STEWARD'S WAY

The life of a Christian steward models the life of Jesus. It is challenging and even difficult, in many respects, yet intense joy comes to those who take the risk to live as Christian stewards. Women and men who seek to live as stewards learn that "all things work for good for those who love God" (Rom 8:28).

After Jesus, we look to Mary as an ideal steward. As the Mother of Christ, she lived her ministry in a spirit of fidelity and service; she responded generously to the call.

We must ask ourselves: Do we also wish to be disciples of Jesus Christ and Christian stewards of our world and our Church?

Central to our human and Christian vocations, as well as to the unique vocation each one of us receives from God, is that we be good stewards of the gifts we possess. God gives us this divine-human workshop, this world and Church of ours.

The Spirit shows us the way.

Stewardship is a part of that journey.

Appendix II

Stewardship and Development in Catholic Dioceses and Parishes

Resource Manual

Contents

Foreword

In 1992, the National Conference of Catholic Bishops approved the publication of a pastoral letter entitled *Stewardship: A Disciple's Response*. This pastoral letter was the work of an Ad Hoc Committee on Stewardship that continues in existence. Since the publication of the pastoral letter, the Ad Hoc Committee has continued to meet on a regular basis to continue its commitment to stewardship education and formation.

This resource manual is the result of the Ad Hoc Committee's efforts to provide useful information and assistance to parishes and dioceses. The Ad Hoc Committee emphasizes that diocesan and parish leadership should begin any program of stewardship education and formation by a prayerful reflection and reading of the pastoral letter itself.

This manual is the result of the efforts of Mr. Daniel Conway of the Archdiocese of Indianapolis and Mr. Vito Napoletano of the Diocese of Orlando. Special thanks must be given to Bishop William McManus, who worked closely with the authors in the development of the final draft. The Ad Hoc Committee is also grateful to Mr. Fred Hofheinz and Lilly Endowment, Inc., for their assistance in the development of this manual.

The Ad Hoc Committee on Stewardship would like to call attention as well to an additional resource manual from the National Catholic Stewardship Council entitled *Stewardship: Disciples Respond*. This resource manual for diocesan and pastoral leaders will complement the work of the Ad Hoc Committee on Stewardship.

Stewardship remains a challenge for people of faith today. Yet, the Ad Hoc Committee on Stewardship believes that a commitment to stewardship will enhance our lives as disciples of Jesus in today's world. May this manual be helpful to all who are looking for ways to make stewardship a reality in the life of the Church.

Most Reverend Thomas J. Murphy, Chair
USCC Ad Hoc Committee on Stewardship
Archbishop of Seattle

I. Introduction

Who is a Christian steward?
One who receives God's gifts gratefully, cherishes and tends them in a responsible and accountable manner, shares them in justice and love with all, and returns them with increase to the Lord.

This comprehensive definition of Christian stewardship headlines the pastoral letter *Stewardship: A Disciple's Response*, which was approved by the National Conference of Catholic Bishops (NCCB) in November 1992.

The definition, rooted in biblical and church tradition, corresponds with Almighty God's decision to entrust to humanity the universe God had created (Gn 1:26-31) and with Jesus Christ's famous parable of the talents (Mt 25:14-36).

For disciples of Christ—everyone who responds to Jesus' invitation, "Come, follow me"—Christian stewardship is an obligation, not an option. Correctly and fully understood, Christian stewardship holds every individual accountable to God for personal care of the universe. At the time of judgment, God will have the right to ask: "What did you do with *my* world?"

Christian stewardship, therefore, applies to everything—all personal talents, abilities, and wealth; the local, national, and worldwide environment; all human and natural resources wherever they are; the economic order; governmental affairs; and even outer space. This stewardship does not tolerate indifference to anything important in God's world.

The pastoral letter describes stewardship as a way of life. It challenges Christians, inspired and guided by the Holy Spirit, to try to see the hand of God in all creation. That calls for time—quality time—and extended perseverance. Stewardship is not easy.

The USCC stewardship pastoral, therefore, is much more than an essay; it is a workbook designed to help diocesan and parish leaders acquire a broad, in-depth comprehension of Christian stewardship. Equally as important as the text itself are copious questions challenging discussion of a total view of stewardship. Though the USCC document is not a "how-to" manual, it has sufficient suggestions for diocesan and parish stewardship committees to develop a wide range of projects and programs worthy of being called "Christian stewardship."

For instance, the environment is critically in need of stewardship attention. Stewardship committees, after completing a full study of the pastoral letter, might consider the improvement of local environmental conditions as one of their first projects. Recycling and conservation can be excellent stewardship endeavors.

There was some disappointment, as well as sharp criticism, when the pastoral letter first appeared in print. Some thought there was a de-emphasis of stewardship as a technique to raise additional funds for financially strapped and needy church institutions. Professional and volunteer fund raisers had hoped that the letter would officially endorse donations of time, talent, and treasure to the Church and to charity as the very heart of Christian stewardship. "What we expected from the bishops," a fund raiser said, "is guidance in how to make donations to the Church a religious experience motivated by the high ideals of stewardship."

Though the pastoral letter insists that Christian stewardship should not focus exclusively on "time, talent, and treasure" for Church and charity, it did not ignore or belittle stewardship's applicability to the Church's financial needs. In fact, the letter is explicit about the relationship between practices of stewardship and the Church's finances. It says, for example, "Sound business practice is a fundamental of good stewardship, and as it relates to church finances, must include the most stringent ethical, legal, and fiscal standards."

The pastoral also says, "Parishioners must accept responsibility for their parishes and contribute generously—both money and personal service—to their programs and projects. Only by living as generous stewards of these local Christian communities, their parishes, can Catholics of the United States hope to make them the vital sources of faith-filled Christian dynamism they are meant to be."

Regarding stewardship's relevance to diocesan finances, the pastoral letter has forthright advice. "The same spirit of personal responsibility in which a Catholic approaches his or her parish should extend to the diocese and be expressed in essentially the same ways: generous material support and self-giving. As in the case of a parish, too, lay Catholics ought to have an active role in the oversight of the stewardship of pastoral leaders and administration at the diocesan level. Indeed, the spirit and practice of stewardship should extend to other local churches and to the universal Church—to the Christian community and to one's sisters and brothers in Christ everywhere—and be expressed in deeds and service and mutual support."

As faithful disciples of the Lord Jesus, Catholics will find the needed religious motivation for a complete commitment to stewardship. Such stewardship will help them respond to the many appeals for the donations of their time, treasure, and talent to the Church and to charity. On the other hand, involvement only in the time, talent, and treasure pattern will not necessarily lead to a full faith in all that Christian stewardship asks and expects of disciples of Jesus. A real steward is a donor to the Church and charity, but not every contributor is a steward in the full sense of the word.

The USCC Stewardship Committee is confident that this resource manual will help dioceses and parishes conduct "time, talent, and treasure" appeals for Church and charity that reflect the ideals of stewardship set forth in the USCC pastoral letter.

STEWARDSHIP AND DEVELOPMENT

When the USCC approved the pastoral letter, the Ad Hoc Committee on Stewardship promised to follow the publication of *Stewardship: A Disciple's Response* with resources to help dioceses and parishes with stewardship education and formation. The Ad Hoc Committee also wanted to respond to growing financial needs in the Church. This resource manual for the implementation of stewardship and development programs has been written for diocesan bishops and their staffs, pastors and parish teams, and lay leaders. The resource manual is a companion to the pastoral letter. For this reason, the resource manual will be of no help, and might be misleading, to persons who have not first read, studied, and discussed the pastoral letter itself.

By design, the principles in this resource manual are general and flexible. They are not a detailed blueprint for stewardship education and formation, fund raising, or diocesan and parish financial management. Hopefully, individual parishes and dioceses will adapt these principles to reflect differences of size, economic circumstance, regional and cultural diversity, and local customs. However, it is important to preserve the basic principles of the pastoral letter *Stewardship: A Disciple's Response* in every local adaptation. This resource manual offers helpful suggestions in the following areas:

1. Developing stewardship education and formation programs for adults, youth, and children

2. Planning and implementing diocesan and parish stewardship and development programs

3. Cultivating, training, and recognizing gifts of time and talent

4. Using stewardship principles to solicit gifts of treasure for annual, capital, and endowment purposes in parishes and dioceses

STEWARDSHIP AS A FAITH RESPONSE

With the publication of *Stewardship: A Disciple's Response*, the word *stewardship* took on a fresh meaning in the Catholic Church in America. By endorsing the concept of stewardship as a "faith response," the bishops of the United States emphasized that the publication of the pastoral letter was not simply to raise money, as important as this may be, for carrying out the mission of the Church. *Stewardship: A Disciple's Response* is an educational tool for bishops, pastors, and other church leaders who wish to invite, and challenge, all members of the Catholic community to accept their baptismal responsibility "to place their gifts, their resources, their selves at God's service in and through the Church." Thus, while emphasizing that stewardship (as a faith response) means more than raising money, the pastoral letter also enables Catholic organizations throughout the United States to develop new strategies for soliciting gifts of time, talent, and treasure that are faithful to the stewardship principles outlined in *Stewardship: A Disciple's Response*.

USING THE PASTORAL LETTER ON STEWARDSHIP

How can bishops, pastors, and other church leaders successfully use the pastoral letter on stewardship to help recruit and train volunteers and to solicit gifts for ongoing programs, capital improvements, and endowments?

First and foremost, by making stewardship a personal commitment as well as a priority for the diocese, parish, or other church-related organization.

Second, by making sure that all members of their leadership teams (staff and volunteers) understand and make a commitment to the concept of stewardship as a faith response.

Third, by evaluating current development and fund-raising practices and replacing them, as necessary, with programs and activities that incorporate stewardship principles and reflect the highest professional standards.

In the final analysis, successful stewardship and development programs in parishes, dioceses, and other church-sponsored organizations will result from the following:

1. The personal involvement of many people (bishop, pastor, staff, volunteers, and the entire Catholic community)

2. A commitment of time, effort, financial resources, and prayer to the process of stewardship education and formation

3. A willingness to trust that if stewardship is taught and accepted as a faith response, urgently needed human, physical, and financial resources will follow.

II. Education and Formation for Stewardship

A MAJOR PRIORITY

Every diocese and parish should make education and formation for stewardship a major priority. This is vitally important today because (1) it helps individuals, families, and communities better understand what it means to follow Jesus in an affluent, consumer culture, and (2) it establishes an appropriate, scriptural basis for responding to the Church's growing need for human, physical, and financial resources.

A LIFELONG PROCESS

Stewardship involves a lifelong process of study, reflection, prayer, and action. To make stewardship a way of life for individuals, families, parishes, and dioceses requires a change of heart and a new understanding of what it means to follow Jesus without counting the cost. This conversion of mind and heart will not happen overnight, but, as always, the Holy Spirit is at work in the Church today. Those parishes and dioceses that embrace the theology and practice of stewardship are beginning to see a change of attitude on the part of clergy, religious, and lay people.

A SOLID FOUNDATION

A comprehensive approach to stewardship education and formation is essential if diocesan and parish communities truly wish to make stewardship a way of life for individuals, families, and communities. Increased offertory and fund-raising programs that bypass stewardship education and formation must be more than a "jump start" to financial giving. Such programs could separate church funding from its vital connection to Christian discipleship. As dioceses, parishes, and other church-related organizations seek to develop urgently needed human, physical, and financial resources, they need encouragement to make sure that their efforts have a solid foundation, which only fully developed stewardship programs can provide.

THE ROLE OF THE BISHOP OR PASTOR IN FORMATION AND EDUCATION FOR STEWARDSHIP

A bishop's or pastor's prayerful meditations on Christian stewardship should precede the start of a diocesan or parish stewardship program. Prayer becomes a potent and precious resource for the process because the primary objective in stewardship education is always a renewal of commitment to Christian discipleship. To be successful, stewardship education requires the bishop or pastor to make a complete, constant, personal, and official commitment to stewardship as a constitutive element of Christian discipleship. A bishop or pastor who does not have a solid conviction about the importance of stewardship will give only half-hearted support to the stewardship programs of his diocese or parish. The results will reflect this lack of total commitment.

THE IMPORTANCE OF COLLABORATIVE LEADERSHIP

The bishop or pastor should convene a stewardship committee (or similar group of advisors) to join him in a serious study of the pastoral letter on stewardship. He should spend quality time with the discussion and study items for each chapter. This committee should discuss *Stewardship: A Disciple's Response* in light of diocesan and parish realities and in the context of the many economic, political, and social issues facing individuals, families, and communities today. The bishop or pastor should personally introduce the theology of stewardship to the leadership team (staff and volunteers, clergy, religious, and lay). He should call upon them to join him in prayerful reflection, study, and discussion of the stewardship pastoral's themes and convictions.

With the assistance of his stewardship committee, the bishop or pastor should establish a series of educational initiatives at the diocesan and parish levels that would encourage all members of the Catholic community to read, study, and discuss the pastoral letter. In addition, it would be good to encourage all members of the Catholic community to meditate on stewardship themes and to pray for the grace to follow Jesus as mature Christian disciples, without counting the cost.

MODEL STEWARDSHIP PROGRAMS

In addition to its broader educational responsibilities, the diocesan or parish stewardship committee should have the responsibility to make sure that all leadership development and fund-raising efforts are consistent with, and reinforce, the theology and practice of stewardship as outlined in the pastoral letter and this manual. Diocesan and parish stewardship committees should also examine and discuss various approaches to stewardship in different regions of the country. No single approach to stewardship "fits" all parishes and dioceses. In fact, as long as basic principles are honored, the more diversity, the better it may be for successful stewardship education and formation of adults, youth, and children throughout the United States.

Adults

Dioceses and parishes serious about making stewardship a way of life for individuals, families, and communities of faith will include stewardship themes in all adult formation and education programs. There are important scriptural and theological connections linking religious education, evangelization, and catechesis on the Church's social teaching with teaching stewardship as a disciple's response. Adult initiation processes, Bible study groups, and other adult education classes should explore and discuss these connections. In addition, diocesan and parish fund-raising efforts (annual appeals, capital campaigns, and planned-giving programs) should always include educational materials designed to help adults better understand the principles and practices associated with good stewardship of time, talent, and treasure.

Leaders in the fields of religious education, evangelization, vocations, lay ministry development, and stewardship education at national, diocesan, and parish levels should develop stewardship educational resources. These resources could emphasize the integration of stewardship themes into all aspects of the education and formation of adult Christians, as well as within all levels of Catholic education.

Youth

Opportunities for learning about (and sharing) their gifts of time, talent, and treasure should be integrated into all educational programs and formation activities sponsored by parishes, schools, and dioceses for youth. This includes study and discussion of the pastoral letter *Stewardship: A Disciple's Response* in religion classes (both in and out of school) and the integration of stewardship themes into other subjects (e.g., environmental studies). In addition, opportunities for Christian service provided by parishes, schools, or dioceses should allow time for reflection and discussion of the stewardship implications of these activities.

Children

The lifelong process of stewardship education and formation begins at home in the domestic church and extends to parish and school religious education programs. Children should be taught the basic themes of Christian discipleship and stewardship. There should be appropriate opportunities to practice stewardship values, including generous sharing of time, talent, and treasure, as well as care for the environment and accountability for our use of all God's gifts. In recent years, a variety of resources for introducing children to the basic principles of Christian stewardship have become available. Pastoral leaders and religious educators should adapt these programs to the needs of individual parishes, schools, and families so that the theology of stewardship becomes an integral part of our children's religious education and formation.

III. Stewardship and Development

Development and fund-raising programs sponsored by dioceses, parishes, schools, and other church-related organizations should complement effective stewardship programs. No development activity should conflict with stewardship efforts in the diocese or parish. Instead, as a result of careful planning, there will be new opportunities for people to practice good stewardship by participating in the mission and ministries of their Church.

The basic elements of a parish or diocesan development program are (1) **a spiritually based plan** with a mission statement, specific goals and objectives, and priorities for funding; (2) **a communications program** that specifies how the diocese, parish, school, or agency will regularly communicate its mission, goals, and funding needs to various internal and external publics; and (3) **a fund-raising program based on stewardship and development principles** that outlines how the diocese, parish, school, or agency will identify prospective donors, build strong relationships, and solicit gifts for current programs, capital needs, and endowments. To be successful, each of these three elements must be carefully coordinated with stewardship education efforts and other fund-raising activities (e.g., annual appeals or capital campaigns) at the diocesan and parish levels.

PRINCIPLES FOR GIVING

One of the most frequently asked questions in any program of church support is "How much should I give?" The following suggestions should help dioceses, parishes, schools, and other church-related organizations encourage individuals, families, and communities to make better decisions about giving as a percent of income.

Diocesan and parish stewardship programs should help individuals, families, and communities better understand why, in the context of a total commitment to stewardship that is planned, proportionate, and sacrificial, it is important to set goals for giving. All Christian stewards must consider prayerfully the gifts they have received from God, and they should make a decision (in advance, from the "first fruits" instead of what is left over after other obligations have been met) about what will be given.

Once Christian stewards make this decision, it is suggested that one-half of an individual's or family's commitment of time, talent, and treasure be given to the parish; the other half can then be divided among other worthwhile religious, educational, and charitable organizations. The diocesan annual appeal is one of the opportunities that members of the Catholic community have for giving from the "other half" of their annual stewardship commitments, and many dioceses suggest 1 percent of a family's net income as a guideline for giving to the diocesan annual appeal.

The practice of "minimum giving" that parishes sometimes adopt as a means of ensuring that school families contribute to overall school costs is inconsistent with the principles of stewardship that encourage members of the Catholic community to embrace the spirit of "maximum giving" from substance without counting the cost. To be consistent with the principles outlined in the pastoral letter, parishes that currently have minimum giving requirements are encouraged to gradually adopt a stewardship program that avoids any suggestion of "obligation" or "guilt" and, instead, stresses the voluntary contribution of time, talent, and treasure.

Similarly, "increased offertory" and diocesan fund-raising programs whose primary objective is to increase the amount of money contributed to the parish or diocese miss the important connection between stewardship as "a way of life" and the gifts of time, talent, and treasure that individuals freely give to their Church out of gratitude to God for the many blessings received. Parish and diocesan annual giving programs should never place so much emphasis on the need for financial giving that the fuller meaning and context of stewardship would be obscured. For this reason, annual giving programs should always emphasize the ways in which stewardship influences all aspects of a Christian's daily life.

The collection during weekend liturgies can be an excellent opportunity to reinforce stewardship principles. In addition to being an instrument for making financial contributions to the parish, the weekly envelope can serve as a concrete expression of traditional giving that each baptized Christian makes during the celebration of the Eucharist.

ANNUAL GIVING

Successful stewardship and development programs frequently include procedures for encouraging annual commitments of time, talent, and treasure to the parish, diocese, school, and other church-related organizations (e.g., an annual Catholic Charities appeal).

In recent years, annual giving programs have begun to replace special events and other indirect fund-raising activities (including games of chance and social functions) as the primary means of raising money for the ongoing operations of religious and other nonprofit organizations. In parishes and dioceses, this national trend toward annual giving is most often evident through annual "commitment Sundays" in parishes and through the diocesan annual appeal. In addition, a growing number of Catholic schools and other church-related agencies have started annual giving programs.

Successful annual giving programs encourage members of the Catholic community to make annual commitments of their time, talent, and treasure to support the work of the Church. Annual giving programs also promote the concept of pledging (as opposed to one-time gifts), and they encourage donors to fulfill their pledges in time frames (weekly, monthly, quarterly, etc.) that best suit their needs. Moreover, parishes should encourage individuals and families who make weekly pledges to make their pledge payments even when they are not able to attend the weekend liturgy at their parish.

A diocesan or parish annual giving program will be consistent with the principles outlined in *Stewardship: A Disciple's Response* if it is based on, and reinforces, the stewardship themes and convictions outlined in the pastoral letter. Moreover, such programs should encourage individuals, families, and communities to embrace a broader understanding of stewardship as a faith response. To ensure that annual giving programs remain consistent with the principles of stewardship, diocesan and pastoral staffs and volunteers should have significant ongoing opportunities for stewardship education and formation.

CAPITAL CAMPAIGNS

A capital campaign is a carefully planned, well-organized, needs-based program to raise a substantial amount of money within a specific time frame. Capital campaigns are ordinarily conducted to raise funds for major building or renovation projects. Occasionally, a campaign methodology may also be used to develop significant financial resources for other parish purposes (e.g., debt elimination, tuition assistance, or endowment development). In a capital campaign, well-informed and well-trained volunteers visit other members of the diocese or parish to discuss the purpose of the campaign, describe the diocese's or parish's capital needs, and answer questions. They then invite individuals and families to make multi-year commitments to the campaign (in addition to their annual giving to the parish, diocese, or other church-related organization).

Capital campaigns represent one of the many choices that individuals and families have to make gifts of time, talent, and treasure to the Church.

Elements of a Successful Capital Campaign

A successful capital campaign should ordinarily include the following elements:

- **A situation analysis and case statement** that outline the current situation in the parish (strengths, weaknesses, opportunities, threats) and make the case for major funding needs. This phase of pre-campaign planning is greatly assisted if the diocese or parish has an up-to-date pastoral plan.

- **A communications program** that seeks to help all members of the diocese or parish understand, accept, and make a commitment to the purposes for which the campaign is being conducted. Ideally, the communications plan will include (1) personal conversations with key individuals and groups; (2) meetings with staff, volunteers, and others as appropriate; (3) printed and audiovisual materials that state the case and show how diocesan or parish needs will be met; and (4) regular reports that keep members of the diocese or parish informed at all stages of the campaign. It is essential that this communications effort involve *listening* as well as talking. Major mistakes can be avoided if, at an early stage in campaign planning, diocesan and parish leaders are able to listen carefully to the concerns and suggestions of those who will be asked to participate in the campaign as volunteers or as donors. An openness to make reasonable changes in the case or in the campaign plans will go a long way toward creating a positive atmosphere for the campaign's success.

- **Identification of major gift prospects** for the capital campaign (and the development of pledge range charts showing the number of major gift prospects and range of gift amounts that are needed) should be initiated as part of the communications phase of the project. This will ensure that those identified as major gift prospects will have an opportunity to participate in this important communications phase of the campaign. This phase of the capital campaign should raise awareness about stewardship as a "faith response." It should also provide major gift prospects with significant opportunities for participation in and support of the mission and ministries of the Church.

- **Committed leadership.** The success of an intensive fund-raising campaign depends on the active involvement of the bishop or pastor, key diocesan and parish staff members, the appropriate consultative bodies (e.g., pastoral council, finance council, and stewardship committee) and other groups as appropriate. In addition, there will be a need to recruit strong volunteer leaders to help plan and implement the campaign.

- **A detailed, well-organized campaign plan.** A successful capital campaign requires careful planning and discipline. Campaign planning starts with the situation analysis and includes the gathering of background materials, financial projections, and other important data. Once these resources have been assembled and a case statement has been drafted and communicated to prospective volunteers and donors (as described above), the diocese or parish is ready to undertake a feasibility study, the process normally used to determine whether an organization has the resources (and the commitment) necessary to raise the desired funds.

If the feasibility study results are positive, the diocese or parish is ready to recruit volunteer solicitors, establish detailed procedures and strict timelines, and develop the necessary procedures for cultivating prospects, soliciting gifts, and recording, acknowledging, and collecting campaign pledges.

Dioceses and parishes that seek to raise more than $1 million in a capital campaign should consider obtaining professional fund-raising counsel to conduct a feasibility study and/or supervise the organization and implementation of the campaign. Before engaging professional counsel, dioceses and parishes should interview three or more firms (including the person who will be designated as campaign director) and contact the references provided by each firm. Careful advance screening can help dioceses and parishes learn from the experiences of others and avoid costly and time-consuming mistakes in their choice of professional counsel.

Campaign Timetables

Campaign timetables should be planned that do not conflict with parish or diocesan stewardship programs or annual appeals. In consideration of the many demands that are made on diocesan and parish staff and volunteers, it may be advisable to combine a capital campaign with the diocese's or parish's annual giving program. When this is the case, extraordinary care must be taken to make sure that prospective volunteers and donors know why the two efforts are being combined. In addition, in a combined annual and capital campaign it is especially important to emphasize that stewardship involves gifts of time and talent as well as gifts of treasure.

Stewardship and the Capital Campaign

A diocesan or parish capital campaign will be consistent with the principles outlined in *Stewardship: A Disciple's Response* if the campaign plans and procedures respect the themes and convictions of the bishops' pastoral letter and if the campaign materials and other communications reinforce the teaching and practice of stewardship as a way of life. To ensure that a capital campaign is based on, and reinforces, a diocese's or parish's stewardship education program, campaign staff and volunteers should have a thorough acquaintance with the theology and practice of stewardship before campaign plans are designed or implemented.

PLANNED GIVING

The term "planned giving" is now commonly used to describe commitments made by donors to transfer capital assets (including cash, stock, certificates of deposit, real estate, or other forms of personal property) to a qualified religious, educational, or charitable organization. Most of the time, a planned gift is made by means of a formal agreement or contract and the principal or income from the gift is not available to the organization until the terms of the agreement are fulfilled (usually at the death of the donor or spouse). Planned gifts are normally made from the contributor's accumulated assets as part of an overall estate plan. In addition to the normal benefits of charitable giving, planned gift agreements frequently result in tax advantages or other income benefits to the donor.

The most common form of planned gift is a bequest provision in a will. Other forms of planned giving include charitable trust agreements, gifts of real estate or insurance, charitable gift annuities, and various combinations of these individual agreements (technically known as "deferred gift agreements").

Characteristics

The most distinctive characteristics of planned giving are the following:

- Gifts are made from capital assets in contrast to outright gifts that are normally made from the donor's current income.
- The donor's personal and financial objectives are of primary concern in the decision whether to make a planned gift and what form of planned gift agreement to choose.
- Depending on what form of planned gift agreement is chosen, the organization designated as the beneficiary may have to assume administrative and/or fiscal responsibilities (which would not ordinarily be the case in an outright gift).

As a result of the growing awareness of the importance of endowment as an essential source of support for religious, educational, and charitable organizations, a natural affinity exists between planned giving and endowment development. Because planned gifts are usually gifts from the donor's accumulated assets, it is not unusual for the donor to prefer some form of endowment or capital purpose that will "preserve" the gift in perpetuity.

Planned Giving Seminars and Educational Programs

Many dioceses and parishes now sponsor seminars and other educational programs for individuals and families interested in learning more about planned giving. Frequently, these educational programs are conducted by local attorneys and other professionals who are knowledgeable in this increasingly complex field and who understand the special requirements of church law. Copies of informational brochures and other planned giving resources are available from the National Catholic Stewardship Council and from firms that specialize in marketing and training for planned giving.

Efforts to provide individuals and families with information about planned giving should be integrated into the diocese's or parish's overall stewardship education program. If properly presented as a means of exercising responsible stewardship of their accumulated assets and as an opportunity to make a distinctive contribution to the mission and ministries of the Church, an educational program designed to promote planned giving can be a double service to church members. It can remind them of their overall stewardship responsibility and, at the same time, provide very practical suggestions on how to increase income, save taxes, and contribute to the Church.

Personal contact with planned gift prospects by a representative of the Church who is knowledgeable in the field of planned giving and who is sensitive to the prospects' needs is the best way to encourage planned gifts. It can also be a significant service to individuals and couples who need assistance in estate planning.

Legal Agreements

Because many planned gifts include agreements that legally bind the beneficiary or that may require administrative or fiscal management, all dioceses, parishes, schools, and other church-related organizations should check with the appropriate church authority before signing any agreements or contracts that would legally bind the organization under the provision of civil or church law.

Endowment Funds

Parishes and schools should not set up separate legal entities for endowment purposes without first receiving permission from their local bishop. A growing number of dioceses have now established diocesan foundations whose primary purpose is to acquire, manage, and invest endowment funds for the benefit of parishes, schools, and other church-related organizations. In these foundations, endowments are managed by investment professionals under the supervision of the local bishop. Individual funds are commingled to maximize the benefit to all. For more information about endowment funds, dioceses and parishes are encouraged to contact the National Catholic Stewardship Council or the Diocesan Fiscal Managers' Conference.

IV. Promoting Gifts of Time, Talent, and Treasure to the Parish and Diocese: Seven Steps to Success

The mission and ministries of the Church in the United States require the personal participation in and financial support of the Catholic people. The following suggestions are intended as a seven-step process (or checklist) to help bishops, pastors, and their staffs and volunteers successfully promote gifts of time, talent, and treasure to the parish and diocese in a manner consistent with the theology of stewardship and principles of effective development.

STEP 1: PERSONAL WITNESS

Since stewardship is a way of life, and not simply a program of church support, the most important ingredient in any effort to encourage giving of time, talent, and treasure is the personal witness of individuals (clergy, religious, and lay) who have experienced a change of heart as a result of their commitment to stewardship. For this reason, parishes and dioceses are strongly encouraged to ground their stewardship and development programs in the personal witness of the bishop, pastor, parish or diocesan staff, and volunteers. An example of this type of personal witness would be for the presider at a liturgy to make a financial contribution or complete a commitment card for time, talent, or resources.

Parish stewardship programs currently in use in parishes and dioceses throughout the United States provide excellent examples of clergy and lay witness talks that can be offered during the liturgies leading up to a stewardship or commitment weekend. To ensure that stewardship is seen as more than simply the parish's annual giving program, witness talks on stewardship themes should also be offered at various times throughout the year. Similarly, diocesan annual giving programs and other diocesan events should include opportunities for personal witness on the part of the bishop and others to the importance of stewardship as a faith response. It is also important that parish leaders present the parish financial report at a different time, preferably a few months prior to the sacrificial giving presentation.

STEP 2: COMMITMENT OF LEADERSHIP

The personal commitment of the bishop or pastor is absolutely necessary for the success of diocesan and parish stewardship and development efforts. In addition, wherever possible, parishes and dioceses should have active stewardship committees whose members include a representative group of pastoral and lay leaders willing to pray, discuss, learn, and lead.

The leadership team commissioned by the bishop or pastor should be responsible for (1) stewardship formation and educational programs in the diocese or parish, and (2) oversight of the parish's or diocese's efforts to promote gifts of time, talent, and treasure for annual, capital, and endowment purposes. Professional staff and/or consultants should be employed where appropriate and where diocesan or parish resources permit. As in all aspects of church life, the collaborative leadership and active involvement of many people are essential to the success of parish and diocesan stewardship efforts.

STEP 3: HOSPITALITY, EVANGELIZATION, AND OUTREACH

Communities known for the vitality of their faith and for the quality of their service to people in need invariably inspire others to participate in their ministries and to be generous in their financial support. With this in mind, parishes and dioceses that seek to promote gifts of time, talent, and treasure to support the mission and ministries of the Church should first demonstrate that they are welcoming communities with a commitment to preaching the Gospel and serving the needs of others.

Parishes and dioceses should not make commitments to hospitality, evangelization, and outreach simply because this will enhance their ability to recruit volunteers or raise money. These activities should be the natural outgrowth of a parish's or diocese's mission. However, dioceses and parishes that seek to increase participation or to raise additional funds would do well to look to the effectiveness of their efforts to welcome, evangelize, and serve.

As an integral part of their commitment to stewardship as a way of life, parish and diocesan leaders should initiate and implement stewardship projects unrelated to the Church itself, e.g., conservation of natural resources, environmental improvements, advocacy projects to benefit the poor and needy, custody of family values, etc. In addition, as a witness to the value of generous giving that is not based on obligation or need, dioceses and parishes should try to make donations of time, talent, and treasure to people and causes (in their local communities and throughout the world) that are over and above their participation in assessments and second collections.

STEP 4: COMMUNICATION AND EDUCATION

All the stewardship and development programs currently in use in dioceses and parishes throughout the United States require the use of one or more communications media. Printed materials, audiovisuals, telemarketing programs, computerized tracking and record keeping, and other contemporary communications instruments now complement letters from the bishop or pastor, witness talks, bulletin announcements, posters, and other traditional means of communication.

Given the competition that exists today for people's time and attention, parishes and dioceses that wish to be successful in stewardship and development must pay careful attention to the effectiveness of their communications. Especially since most dioceses and parishes are working with very limited communications budgets, the choices that are made about how to most effectively "tell our story" or "make our case" can be crucial to success. With this in mind, parishes and dioceses are urged to seek the assistance of qualified communications professionals (staff and volunteers) to develop communications plans that will make the best possible use of available resources.

STEP 5: RECRUITING, TRAINING, AND RECOGNIZING GIFTS OF TIME AND TALENT

The demands made on people's time and energy make it more important than ever to recruit, train, and recognize gifts of time and talent for the parish or diocese. Active recruitment of volunteers is essential to the parish's or diocese's stewardship of its own human and financial resources because the active involvement of individuals, families, and communities in the mission and ministries of the Church is one of the surest signs of the health and vitality of any faith community.

To make sure that the time and talent of volunteers are respected and used wisely, dioceses and parishes should invest staff time and budget resources in the training and continuing education of volunteers. They should also find appropriate ways to recognize and celebrate the precious gifts of time and talent that people contribute to the Church on behalf of the mission of the Church.

New educational resources and training materials are needed to help parishes and dioceses improve their efforts to recruit, train, and recognize volunteers. To ensure that gifts of time and talent receive their proper emphasis and are not overshadowed by efforts to secure gifts of treasure, careful attention should be paid to this increasingly important aspect of a total stewardship education program.

STEP 6: STEWARDSHIP OF TREASURE

Parishes and dioceses that wish to encourage financial gifts for ongoing programs, capital needs, and endowment should look first to steps 1 to 5 above.

- Has the parish or diocese effectively witnessed to the value of stewardship as a way of life?
- Is the leadership fully committed to stewardship and development?
- Are individuals and families in this diocese or parish actively involved in ministries of hospitality, evangelization, and service?
- How effective are parish or diocesan communications?
- And, finally, are gifts of time and talent really welcome, or does the parish or diocese unwittingly send a message that it only cares about money?

The parish or diocese that can honestly evaluate itself on these questions with a positive result will be in an excellent position to encourage gifts of treasure to support the mission and ministries of the Church. Building on this kind of solid foundation, the diocese or parish should employ fund-raising methods that respect and reinforce stewardship themes of gratitude, accountability, generosity, and returning to the Lord with increase.

Within a total stewardship context, parishes and dioceses should not hesitate to use the best available ethically sound fund-raising practices to ask the Catholic people to make financial contributions that are planned, proportionate, and sacrificial. Provided that the basic approach is consistent with the theology and practice of stewardship, the principles and techniques of professional fund raising can be extremely helpful to the overall stewardship and development efforts of the parish or diocese.

STEP 7: ACCOUNTABILITY

Success in the stewardship and development efforts of a parish or diocese requires a visible commitment to accountability. This commitment includes accountability for the full range of parish or diocesan activities—from the way decisions are made and carried out by diocesan or parish personnel to the way money is collected, managed, and used. Indeed, accountability is fundamental to good stewardship.

Parishes and dioceses are urged to prepare annual reports of their stewardship. These reports should be prepared in a manner that promotes understanding of the relationship between the ministries of the Church and the financial affairs of the parish or diocese. Church leaders should also use the annual report to render an account of their stewardship of human resources (personnel policies, just compensation, etc.), and their stewardship of church property and facilities.

A visible commitment to accountability will be reflected in the leadership styles and attitudes of the bishop, pastor, and all who have responsibilities for the human, physical, and financial resources of the diocese or parish. Like personal witness, a commitment to accountability is essential to building a solid foundation for a diocesan or parish stewardship program.

The seven steps suggested here are not intended to be an exhaustive list of all of the programs or activities that are required for success in promoting gifts of time, talent, and treasure. However, the experience of parishes and dioceses in many different regions of the country shows that if these seven principles are honored, the Catholic people will respond generously to the invitation to participate in the mission and ministries of their Church.

A Final Word: Gratitude to All Involved in the Ministry of Stewardship

This resource manual outlines well the challenge that parishes and dioceses are trying to address in responding to the pastoral letter, *Stewardship: A Disciple's Response*, issued by the National Conference of Catholic Bishops in November 1992. However, one final word needs to be added. It is the word of gratitude and appreciation to all those involved in the ministry of stewardship and development. We need to appreciate the women and men for whom stewardship is a ministry and a vocation. We need to recognize the gift of volunteer time, effort, and energy that so many people generously share with their dioceses and parishes.

In a special way, we acknowledge the pastoral leadership of our parishes and dioceses—bishops, pastors, pastoral ministers, and countless others. Their own commitment to stewardship creates the environment that will help our faith communities continue the mission and ministry of Jesus in today's world. To all those whose lives reflect the challenge of a disciple of Jesus through a commitment to stewardship, thank you for your witness of faith and generosity.

In the words of St. Paul to the Philippians,

> "I give thanks to my God at every remembrance of you, praying always with joy in my every prayer for all of you, because of your partnership for the gospel from the first day until now. I am confident of this, that the one who began a good work in you will continue to complete it until the day of Christ Jesus." (Phil 1:3-6)

Key Concepts

The following definitions of key concepts and terms for stewardship, philanthropy, development, and fund raising are offered in order to identify the similarities and differences among these important concepts that are too often used interchangeably.

ACCOUNTABILITY

Central to our understanding of stewardship and development is the concept of accountability. Dioceses, parishes, schools, and other church-related organizations that seek to develop urgently needed human and financial resources need to show that their programs and services truly "make a difference" in meeting the spiritual, educational, and social needs of the people they serve. They also need to give evidence of their long-term stability and growth potential to encourage investment. This is a basic requirement of stewardship and development—to render an account of the organization's use of the time, talent, and treasure entrusted to its care. As the demand for charitable giving grows (and competition increases), accountability will become an even more important indicator of whether an organization is "worthy of investment."

COMMUNICATIONS

Making sure that the members of a parish or diocesan family are well informed in our world of mass communications and increasingly sophisticated information technology requires much more than articles in the diocesan newspaper, bulletin announcements, form letters, or occasional newsletters.

Quality communications is the result of hard work and careful planning. It also requires a significant financial investment by the diocese, parish, school, or other church-related organization. Today more than ever, important matters need to be communicated as personally as possible through individual and group meetings, personal letters and phone calls, and a full array of printed, electronic, and audiovisual support materials. In addition, given the mobility of our people today, informational items should be communicated frequently and in a variety of ways, so that those who miss one information source can still be reached through other sources.

If the desired outcome of our communications efforts is a community of people who understand, accept, and are committed to the mission and goals of the diocese, parish, school, or agency, we must develop forms of communication that can inform, motivate, and invite people to participate in our mission. As a Catholic community about to enter the new millennium, the communications opportunities and challenges that are being presented to us are staggering. The way we respond to these challenges and opportunities will have significant consequences for evangelization, religious education, and all our stewardship and development activities.

DEVELOPMENT

Development refers to a program of planned or systematic growth in which a religious, educational, or charitable organization reaches out to its various publics and invites them to invest in its current and long-range goals. According to this definition, a successful development program involves the coordination and integration of three essential functions: planning, communications, and fund raising.

FUND RAISING

Unlike stewardship, which is a way of life involving all aspects of an individual Christian's daily life, fund raising is a very specific set of activities designed to support the mission and goals of a diocese, parish, or other church-related organization. Fund raising is a discipline. It is a planned and organized effort to find potential volunteers and donors, to build strong relationships, and to ask for gifts of time, talent, and treasure to support the fund-raising organization's specific mission and goals. Although there are many different kinds of fund-raising activities, efforts to raise money for voluntary organizations fall into two main categories: direct fund raising and indirect fund raising.

Direct fund raising

Prospective donors are directly asked to make a contribution of their time, their talent, and/or their treasure for the benefit of a religious, educational, or charitable organization. Direct fund-raising activities are normally organized into an annual appeal for unrestricted funds to support current programs and activities, special appeals for short-term or special projects, capital campaigns for building or other major projects, and planned giving (wills, trusts, real estate, etc.) that is sometimes associated with endowments.

The primary advantage of direct fund raising is its emphasis on building a strong, personal relationship between the donor and the organization that is seeking support. In each of the direct fund-raising efforts mentioned above, the organization seeking support must do careful planning, communicate its case in compelling and convincing ways, and "ask for the gift" in appropriate and effective ways.

Although most voluntary organizations use some combination of direct and indirect fund-raising methods, growing financial needs and increasing competition for the fund-raising dollar have caused organizations to rely less on indirect fund raising and to turn to more effective and efficient direct fund-raising methods.

Indirect fund raising

Prospective donors are asked to purchase goods or services (magazines, candy, picnics, benefit dinners, etc.), and net profits are used to benefit a religious, educational, or charitable organization. These forms of fund raising often have very positive social benefits (e.g., building a stronger sense of community among staff and volunteers). However, the activities themselves do not necessarily build strong relationships between individual donors and the organization seeking support. Generally speaking, indirect fund-raising efforts are more effective at raising smaller amounts of money (often at little or no cost) than they are at raising substantial funds. Thus, if the goal is $500, an indirect fund-raising activity (e.g., bake sale) might be the perfect method. If, however, the goal is $50,000, an enormous amount of time, effort, and energy may be required to achieve this goal through indirect means.

GENEROSITY AND SELF-GIVING

In addition to the importance of accountability, what stewardship and development programs have in common is the basic underlying value or conviction that self-giving is good for the spiritual health and vitality of the individual, family, or community. In addition, all professional, ethically based fund-raising programs recognize that the needs of the human family compel individuals and groups to reach out beyond their individual homes, neighborhoods, or communities to help others who are in need and to make contributions to the common good that would not be possible otherwise.

As in any aspect of Christian life, we sometimes take the value of self-giving for granted, and we forget that raising funds should never be an end in itself. Thus, while it is important to keep in mind the significant differences that exist among the concepts of stewardship and development, it is also essential that we understand that these concepts are not compatible with tactics that seek to raise money through excessive pressure or guilt and are clearly incompatible with deception or fraud. In fact, when properly understood and practiced, the concepts of stewardship and development represent a tradition of generosity and service that should make any Christian and any citizen proud.

PHILANTHROPY

Philanthropy can be defined as any voluntary action that benefits human society. Literally, philanthropy (which means "love of humanity") refers to a caring disposition that prompts individuals and communities to give of themselves with no other motive than the benefit of others. Like stewardship, philanthropy includes the concept of volunteerism, that is, gifts of "wisdom and work" as well as gifts of wealth. Among the distinguishing features of American culture are the philanthropic traditions that have developed in all regions of the United States in response to community needs. In recent years, as government support has declined, education, social services, the arts, and many voluntary organizations have increasingly had to rely on the private philanthropy of individuals, corporations, and foundations. As a result, organizations like Independent Sector have been formed to remind all Americans that maintaining our country's tradition of philanthropy is not just the responsibility of a wealthy elite but is a civic duty to be shared by all. In the Greek Orthodox tradition, "philanthropy" is understood in a religious context and is very similar to our concept of stewardship.

PLANNING

To be successful in developing the human and financial resources needed to carry out its mission, a diocese, parish, school, or agency needs to have a plan. The purpose of the plan is to set direction by answering the following fundamental questions:

- Who are we? What is our primary mission?
- What makes us distinctive as a diocese, parish, or other church-related organization? What values do we choose to emphasize as characteristic of "what we stand for"?
- What do we want to do? What are our major long-term goals?
- How can we accomplish our goals? What are our main objectives?
- What specific action steps will we take to carry out our objectives? How do we measure our success or failure (accountability)?

A plan that can simply and honestly answer each of these fundamental questions will accomplish two important objectives: (1) it will set direction for all the programs and activities of the diocese, parish, or other church-related organization, and (2) it will guide all stewardship and development activities by setting the agenda for communications and establishing priorities for fund raising.

ROLE OF LEADERSHIP

Successful stewardship and development programs require the active involvement of *all* of an organization's leaders (bishop, pastor, and other church leaders) working together as a team. As traditionally defined, the successful stewardship and development team requires the participation and interaction of leaders as follows:

- **Executive**
  (bishop, pastor, and other executive staff)
  Responsible for articulating the mission and goals; identifying opportunities for investment; planning; ensuring accountability; and soliciting major gifts.

- **Volunteer Leaders**
  (council or board members; other lay leaders)
  Responsible for providing counsel and guid-

ance on policy; representing community needs and interests to the organization; endorsing programs; validating resource needs; advocating for strong support within the community; and soliciting major gifts.

- **Staff**
  (paid staff, such as diocesan development director, or volunteers)
  Responsible for coordinating all stewardship and development activities, including stewardship educational programs; monitoring and updating long-range plans; developing and implementing communications strategies; organizing fund-raising efforts for annual, capital, and endowment purposes; and soliciting major gifts.

Depending on the size of the diocese, parish, or organization, these three leadership roles (executive, staff, and volunteer) will involve many staff members and volunteers whose active involvement in stewardship education and in various fund-raising programs is essential to the overall success of a development program. What the team concept illustrates is the fact that successful development is never the result of a single person (staff or volunteer) whose job is "to raise money." As an integral part of the stewardship responsibility of a diocese, parish, school, or agency, some aspect of the overall development function should be included in everyone's job description.

STEWARDSHIP

Who is a Christian steward? One who receives God's gifts gratefully, cherishes and tends them in a responsible and accountable manner, shares them in justice and love with others, and returns them with increase to the Lord.

TALENT

If stewardship means taking care of, and sharing, all God's gifts, then stewardship of the gift of talent means nurturing, developing, and using the God-given abilities and characteristics that help to define "who we are" as individual human persons. Most of us know what it means to contribute money or to give away our precious time, but what does it mean to be a good steward of talent? Our talents are the special blessings that each of us has received from a loving Creator who prizes the diversity and abundant variety of all creation. When we volunteer to work for our parish or diocese or to help a neighbor with a difficult chore, what we have to give is much more than our time. We also give something of ourselves, those characteristics that make each of us distinctive as human beings. We call these our "talents," those things that we're good at or that we especially like to do. When we volunteer to help others by sharing our talents with them, we give them something far more precious than our time or money. We give them something of ourselves, an intimate sharing of "who we are" for the good of others.

All of the parishes, schools, agencies, and institutions of the Church in the United States are blessed with thousands of volunteers who share their talents with others. The "time and talent catalogs" that many parishes publish each year describe hundreds of ways that people can and do give of themselves, from visiting the sick to frying fish, from counseling youth to serving on parish committees. These gifts of self are every bit as important as the financial contributions we make to support the Church's ministry.

TIME

A true understanding of stewardship begins with taking care of and sharing the gift of time. Stewardship of time involves the realization that none of us "owns" time. Each of us is given only so much of it, and planning a careful schedule in order to have the time to work, to rest, to play, and to pray is vital in the stewardship of our physical, emotional, spiritual, and intellectual lives.

In a busy society like ours, time is one of the most precious possessions we have. How we spend our time is perhaps the clearest indication of our progress in a life of Christian discipleship.

TREASURE

True stewardship is taking care of and sharing all that we have and all that we are—our time, talents, and treasure. Why is it so important to share our treasure?

Money and all of the things that we possess (our treasure) are gifts from God that we are asked to care for and generously share for our own benefit and the good of others. It is important for us to share our money and all of our material possessions for two reasons: first, because all the good things that God has made (including money) are meant to be shared, and second, because each of us has a *need to give*.

Why do we need to give? We need to give our money to individuals and families in need, to the Church, and to other worthwhile charitable organizations because giving money is good for the soul and because we need to return thanks to a loving God for all of the many blessings each of us has received.

One of the most frequently asked questions in any stewardship educational program is "How much do I have to give?" The answer (from a stewardship perspective) is *nothing*. We don't *have* to give anything. "How much do we want to give?" is the question that stewardship asks. Stewardship is not minimum giving. It is maximum giving. That means giving as much as we can, as often as we can, from the heart as a faith response because we are generous stewards who want to share our time, talent, and treasure with others.

Frequently, in discussions of stewardship (or "sacrificial giving"), reference will be made to "the biblical tithe" (giving 10 percent of income) and other norms that could provide helpful guidelines for generous giving. As disciples of Jesus, each of us has a responsibility to support the Church and to contribute generously to the building up of the Body of Christ. The emphasis in the bishops' pastoral, *Stewardship: A Disciple's Response*, is not on "tithing" (giving a fixed percent of income), but on giving according to our means. In many ways, this is a far more challenging norm. It challenges us to be good stewards not only in how much we give away, but in what we do with all our resources.